Upper Cape & Islands

Bourne
Sandwich
① ②
Barnstable
Mashpee
③
④ Dennis
Yarmouth
⑧
Hyannis
⑦
⑪
⑫
Falmouth
⑤
⑥

1 • Shawme Pond
2 • Sandy Neck Beach
3 • Great Marshes
4 • Hallett's Mill Pond
5 • Salt and Siders Ponds
6 • South Cape Beach
7 • West Dennis Beach
8 • Swan Pond
9 • Felix Neck Wildlife Sanctuary
10 • Rams Pasture
11 • Ashumet Holly Reservation
12 • Crane Reservation

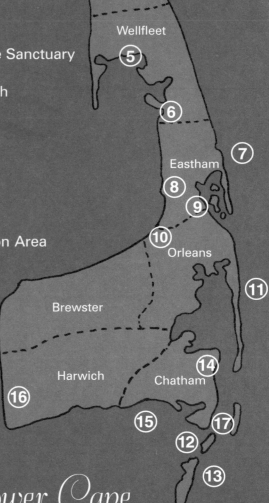

Provincetown
①
②
④
Truro
Wellfleet
⑤
⑥
Eastham
⑦
⑧
⑨
⑩
Orleans
⑪
Brewster
⑭
Harwich
Chatham
⑯
⑮
⑰
⑫
⑬

1 • Race Point Beach
2 • Beech Forest
3 • Pilgrim Heights
4 • Corn Hill
5 • Wellfleet Fish Pier
6 • Wellfleet Bay Wildlife Sanctuary
7 • Coast Guard Beach
8 • First Encounter Beach
9 • Fort Hill
10 • Rock Harbor
11 • Nauset Beach
12 • Morris Island
13 • Monomoy Islands
14 • Chatham Fish Pier
15 • Cockle Cove
16 • Harwich Conservation Area
17 • South Beach

⑨
Martha's Vineyard

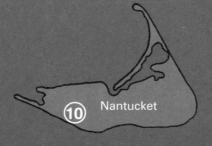

⑩ Nantucket

Lower Cape

⑬

Birds of Cape Cod

And The Islands

Roger S. Everett

With a Foreword by Priscilla Bailey

Schiffer Publishing Ltd

4880 Lower Valley Road, Atglen, PA 19310 USA

Dedication

This book is dedicated to
CORINNE
My wife and best friend
Since June 26, 1948.
She is also an excellent bird spotter.

Cover and book designed by: Bruce Waters
Type set in Bernhard Tango heading font/Adobe Jenson text font

ISBN: 0-7643-2461-6
Printed in China

Published by Schiffer Publishing Ltd.
4880 Lower Valley Road
Atglen, PA 19310
Phone: (610) 593-1777; Fax: (610) 593-2002
E-mail: Info@schifferbooks.com

For the largest selection of fine reference books on this and related subjects, please visit our web site at **www.schifferbooks.com**
We are always looking for people to write books on new and related subjects. If you have an idea for a book please contact us at the above address.

This book may be purchased from the publisher.
Include $3.95 for shipping.
Please try your bookstore first.
You may write for a free catalog.

In Europe, Schiffer books are distributed by
Bushwood Books
6 Marksbury Ave.
Kew Gardens
Surrey TW9 4JF England
Phone: 44 (0) 20 8392-8585; Fax: 44 (0) 20 8392-9876
E-mail: info@bushwoodbooks.co.uk
Free postage in the U.K., Europe; air mail at cost.

Contents

I. Foreword---5

II. In and Around The Yard---8

III. Marshes and Ponds---38

IV. Seashore---71

V. Fields (Managed Lands)---126

VI. Forests---162

VII. Rare Sightings---204

VIII. Closing Words---221

IX. Index---222

Acknowledgments

To Bessie Clifford, whose yard full of birds created the interest that led to my specializing in bird photography.

To the late Wallace Bailey, the late Dick Forster, Blair Nikula and Wayne Petersen for their patience in identifying the birds in my slides and for their assistance in teaching me where to find birds on Cape Cod and the Islands.

To Priscilla Bailey for writing the inspiring Foreword to this book.

To my granddaughter, Jennifer Byrne, for all the typing.

To Mike O'Connor who has alerted me to many wonderful photo opportunities as he passed along sightings people called in to his Birdwatcher's General Store.

I used Roger Tory Peterson's "Field Guide to Eastern Birds" as a reference as I put together this book.

Coverage

There is no intent to include in this book every species ever seen on Cape Cod & the Islands. We are including the most common species that one would expect to see, plus many of the seasonal migrants and a few of the rarer visitors.

There is also no intent to slight anyone's favorite birding spot. The locations included are those that the author most frequently uses for finding and photographing birds.

Prints Available

The author has matted prints available for sale in several sizes, not only of the photos included in this book, but many others. Write for details to: Roger S. Everett, 43 Linnell Landing Road, Brewster, MA 02631

The title page of Edward Howe Forbush's three-volume opus proclaims **BIRDS OF MASSACHUSETTS** in large, bold type; then — much smaller — AND OTHER NEW ENGLAND STATES. Thus a region roughly seven times the size of Massachusetts appears as an also-ran. It suggests a certain provincial conceit, so might our present look at *Birds of Cape Cod & The Islands*. Can a sandy squiggle and a few random lumps — remnants of the Ice Age — have ornithological relevance to the vast continent behind them?

Forbush would tell us yes. His pioneering work, published in 1925, retains stature today as benchmark for regional bird studies expressed with wordsmanship and earthy erudition. As State Ornithologist with the Massachusetts Department of Agriculture from 1908 to 1920, he worked in an optimum of geographical and social influences. Boston was home of the founders of the Massachusetts Audubon in 1896. William Brewster, a resident of Cambridge, founded the Nuttall Ornithological Club, the American Ornithologists' Union, and published in 1906 *Birds of the Cambridge Region*. Over the following decades the aureole reached Cape Cod, Martha's Vineyard, Nantucket, and the nearby islets. Their varied landscapes attract both spectacular numbers of birds and growing ranks of birders — a combination inspiring several publications of annotated checklists — the who-what-where-when of popular bird study.

Of the more then eight hundred species of birds recorded in North America, nearly four hundred have reached this eastern outpost. Among that number, some two hundred regularly pass here on their way to somewhere else — blithe tourists who are among the world's greatest long-distance migrants. Some circle twice yearly from High Arctic to southernmost South America. All are miraculous in their commitment to the command of seasons and hormones.

Another hundred-twenty species regularly breed here. Many of them follow a species-old timetable to arrive in spring, find in the diverse terrain the precise niche necessary to nest and rear their young, then depart. Some dozen species are non-migratory. Their home ground must fulfill the needs of a lifetime.

For some observers the most intriguing birds are the wanderers arriving not by grand design, but by sheerest accident. One such was the Red-footed Falcon (normally ranging Africa and Central Europe) that found its way to Martha's Vineyard in August, 2004. Hundreds of birders and non-birders alike traveled there to see for themselves this first documented occurrence in the Western Hemisphere. Another falcon, the Eurasian Kestrel, caused traffic jams in Chatham in April, 2002. Both species represent, in the extreme, a group of strays observed far beyond their normal range. Is their presence here a failure of their genetic guidance systems? Or can it presage a shift in migration routes or an expansion of breeding range or both — as might be suggested by recent repeated occurrence on Monomoy of Old World visitors like Black-tailed Godwit and Little Stint? For all long-haul migrants, the Cape and Islands offer last hope for land birds carried in the eastward flow of weather toward the sea. And they loom as first obstacle for sea birds blown ashore. For north/south drifters who have miscalculated longitude (from the North Pole, *everything* is south) the region is a beckoning bulge on the continent's edge.

Birds have always traveled along this critical interface of weather systems, land masses, and the sea. And humans have regarded them variously as food, weather indicators, despoilers of crops, and as omens and auguries. Now they are viewed by growing ranks of amateur ornithologists — birders — who are almost as abundant and as varied as the birds they seek. The American Birding Association has 22,000 members and estimates that fifty-one million Americans have some interest in birds. Some want chiefly to become acquainted with neighborhood species, to learn their names and ways, to know their needs and the environment that sustains them. Others strive to see as many different kinds as possible and identify them by color, pattern, shape, size, habitat, and behavior. Still others cherish birds as part of the appealing great outdoors and as monitors of the health of our environment. Avian systems sense the chill of danger long before it penetrates our buffered lives.

Birding Cape Cod goes far back of today's well-equipped and conservation-conscious devotee. "Birder" originally meant one who killed birds, usually for food. Commercial gunners of the nineteenth century shipped to Boston markets the wealth of game from the region's shores and uplands. Many a specimen that furthered the infant science of ornithology went from meat-hook to skinning table to museum tray. So arose the old saw, "What's hit is history; what's missed is mystery." Early naturalists explored this area's abundance with the only technology available to them — notebook, haversack, and gun.

The gap between shotgun naturalist and modern field biologist closed here on Cape Cod in the early years of the twentieth century when Ludlow Griscom proved it possible for a good field biologist to accurately identify living birds in their own environment. He emphasized learning for each species those distinguishing characteristics visible not in the hand but in the field, i.e. *field marks*.

Mr. Griscom perfected his system in the bastions of formal science at the Museum of Natural History in New York and at Harvard University's Museum of Comparative Zoology. From his Cape Cod summer home in Chatham, he encouraged a coterie of young birders who were to lead the new era of popular bird study. Roger Tory Peterson, one of the group, would further revolutionize amateur ornithology with his concept of field guides — compact, graphic illustrations of birds as seen in natural settings. His first field guide, published in 1934, took nature study out of the laboratory and into the pockets of birding enthusiasts, now among outdoor recreation's largest and fastest growing groups.

The book you now hold brings together aspects of field guide, travelogue, and photo-essay on appreciating nature. Most significantly, it features the camera, the tool that replaced the gun in making a permanent record of the ephemeral meeting of bird and bird-observer. It displays the camera's accuracy and immediacy as filtered by artistry. Here the mechanics of fine photography are guided by humane affection — not without humor — for the subject in the lens. Roger Everett shares his personal record of glimpses into nature's wild and beautiful byways tenanted by small lives that tolerate – or endure – our proximity. These, then, are over three hundred birds according to Roger's vision of them, seen with a photographer's eye and a naturalist's heart. What we see in them depends on our own experience. Perhaps we will be led to see clearer in the field and to see better, in terms of insight, concerning our stewardship of their world.

Roger began looking at birds because it was the best excuse for excursions to delightful places. He looked at Brewster on Cape Cod, first as a vacationer; then after 1985 as a resident — except when lured away by the Caribbean, Arizona, and other photogenic places. Long before he knew their names, he delighted in the curious ways of Sanderling on an outer beach, the evanescent glow of Yellow Warblers in apple blossoms. He turned his lens on these new subjects. But what had he recorded? A portrait needs a title. In the process of learning identities, he was hooked by the birding game, the challenge to find and identify. Still, that remains secondary to the satisfaction of capturing an insightful likeness of a wary wild creature whose work-a-day business is to stay out of sight and out of reach of perceived predators such as humans. To do so he uses a Nikon camera, 400mm lens, a two-power teleconverter, and a very sturdy tripod. But he may tell you that his most important equipment is a folding chair. Patience is as necessary as film.

Photographs are presented here by habitat groups rather than as scientists arrange species in presumed order of evolution. A Loon swims near the roots of the mighty Tree of Life and a Goldfinch perches in its topmost twigs, but knowing that will give most of us precious little help in finding one on the morning walk. However, knowledge of habitat requirements is basic to field study. In all aspects of daily life, a bird is tied to the precise environment dictated by its own structure, physiology, and species behavior. "Free as a bird" is appropriate only in the liberal or poetic sense of flight. As landscapes become homogenized suburbia, wildlife diversity dwindles. The more specialized and sensitive give way to the tough adapters. The science of habitat utilization is an aspect of serious ornithology. We might simply remember, while enjoying these avian portraits, that their backgrounds are foregrounds — indeed, the front lines — of the battle to preserve world wildlife.

Roger's sequence of photographs begins with close and personal back yards. It ranges outward through panoramas dearly familiar to some and intriguingly unexplored to others: ponds and marshes; grasslands (of special value because they are the most diminished); woodlands; seashores. Within each group are both familiar species whose reassuring presence proves the passing seasons, and some of the specialties that reward the dedicated searcher who knows the right place and time. This collection of photographs represents the richness of the world of birds and one man's pleasure in making it part of his world. He may show you ways to make it part of yours. Use it to confirm an identification. Apply it as an aid to carving and painting, as incentive to explore a vacation area, to hang a feeder, to create a backyard sanctuary. Use it knowing that these birds are important to this photographer. These careful – and caring – portraits carry an implicit plea for the preservation of the lives and life-styles represented by the birds of Cape Cod and the Islands.

Priscilla H. Bailey
Chatham, Cape Cod
July 2005

II. In and Around the Yard

Year-Round Regulars

Fig. 1. Black-Capped Chickadee
Fig. 2. Black-Capped Chickadee
Fig. 3. Northern Cardinal (Male)
Fig. 4. Northern Cardinal (Male)
Fig. 5. Northern Cardinal (Female)
Fig. 6. Blue Jay
Fig. 7. House Finch (Male)
Fig. 8. House Finch (Female)
Fig. 9. Mourning Dove
Fig. 10. American Goldfinch (Male)
Fig. 11. American Goldfinch
Fig. 12. American Goldfinch
Fig. 13 . Tufted Titmouse
Fig. 14. White-Breasted Nuthatch
Fig. 15. White-Breasted Nuthatch
Fig. 16. Red-Breasted Nuthatch
Fig. 17. Downy Woodpecker
Fig. 18. Hairy Woodpecker
Fig. 19. Red-Bellied Woodpecker (Male)
Fig. 20. Red-Bellied Woodpecker (Female)
Fig. 21. Red-Headed Woodpecker
Fig. 22. Northern Mockingbird
Fig. 23. Northern Mockingbird
Fig. 24. Common Bobwhite (Male)
Fig. 25. American Robin

One of the best and easiest places to see birds on Cape Cod can be in your own yard. This is the best location to photograph birds by constructing a simple blind and allowing the birds to become familiar with it. They soon will be all around you. In our yard we also "plant" a dead tree limb near the feeders that the birds will use as a posing perch for your pictures.

A Cape Cod yard will attract many birds by:

- Setting up feeders for sunflower seed and thistle
- Hanging out suet and putting cracked corn on the ground
- Always having water available year round
- Putting out raisins, oranges and grape jelly
- Planting bushes that have berries
- Being sure there is cover for the birds nearby such as evergreens, bushes or underbrush

Place all the above so it is visible from your home and you can enjoy the entertainment. Do not assume that after a couple of days you have seen all the different species that will come to your yard. Keep watching. Many unusual birds could appear anytime during the year and it is very exciting to find you have a "rare" bird in your own yard. One of the events that led me to become a more serious bird photographer was the arrival of a European finch, called a Brambling, at our feeder in Mansfield, Massachusetts before we moved full-time to the Cape.

Fig. 26. American Robin
Fig. 27. Carolina Wren
Fig. 28. Carolina Wren
Fig. 29. House Sparrow
Fig. 30. House Sparrow (immature)
Fig. 31. White-Throated Sparrow
Fig. 32 . Yellow-Rumped Warbler
Fig. 33. Yellow-Rumped Warbler
Fig. 34. Yellow-Shafted Flicker
Fig. 35. Yellow-Shafted Flicker
Fig. 36. Common Crow
Fig. 37. Eastern Bluebird (Male)
Fig. 38. Eastern Bluebird (Female)

Spring & Summer Visitors

Fig. 39. Gray Catbird
Fig. 40. Baltimore Oriole
Fig. 41. Baltimore Oriole
Fig. 42. Summer Tanager
Fig. 43. Common Grackle
Fig. 44. Brown-Headed Cowbird
Fig. 45. Indigo Bunting
Fig. 46. Rufous-Sided Towhee (Male)
Fig. 47. Rufous-Sided Towhee (Female)
Fig. 48. Ruby-Throated Hummingbird
Fig. 49. Ruby-Throated Hummingbird

Fall and Winter Visitors

Fig. 50. Slate-Colored Junco
Fig. 51. American Tree Sparrow
Fig. 52. Fox Sparrow
Fig. 52A. Pine Siskin

Fig. 1. **BLACK-CAPPED CHICKADEE**. A bundle of energy, always moving, it will come close when you are filling the feeders and will eat everything.

Fig. 2. **BLACK-CAPPED CHICKADEE.** Builds its nest in a small cavity in a dead tree.

Fig. 3. **NORTHERN CARDINAL** (Male). A beautiful bird and everyone's favorite (except bird banders), they come for sunflower seeds. This photo uses the "planted" branch next to the feeders.

Fig. 4. **NORTHERN CARDINAL** (Male). All birds seem to feel more at ease when they blend into a habitat of similar color.

Fig. 5. **NORTHERN CARDINAL** (Female). Always keep bushes near your feeding area so the birds can get under cover quickly.

Fig. 6. **BLUE JAY.** A beautiful but aggressive bird that scatters other birds from the feeding area with its raucous calls.

Fig. 7. **HOUSE FINCH** (Male). A transplant to Cape Cod, this Finch has taken over the sunflower feeders and pushed out the more colorful Purple Finch.

Fig. 8. **HOUSE FINCH** (Female) A rather drab little bird in comparison to its mate.

Fig. 10. **AMERICAN GOLDFINCH** (Male). Thistle
seed will bring this colorful bird to your yard all year.

Fig. 9. **MOURNING DOVE.** A regular at most feeders
that have sunflower seeds and cracked corn.

Fig. 11. **AMERICAN GOLDFINCH.** This could be either a female all year or a male in winter when they look the same.

Fig. 12. **AMERICAN GOLDFINCH.** If you put up a thistle feeder, they will come.

Fig. 13 . **TUFTED TITMOUSE.** A very active bird, it loves sunflower seeds and always in motion, making it difficult to photograph.

Fig. 14. **WHITE-BREASTED NUTHATCH.** Another sunflower eater, it walks down a tree and often hangs upside down when feeding.

Fig. 15. **WHITE-BREASTED NUTHATCH.** Like all other birds that come to your yard, the Nuthatch needs water for drinking and bathing.

Fig. 16. **RED-BREASTED NUTHATCH.** Not as common as the White-Breasted Nuthatch, it can, however, be regular at your suet.

Fig. 17. **DOWNY WOODPECKER.** This will be a regular at your feeder if you put out suet. The male has a red patch on the back of his head.

Fig. 18. **HAIRY WOODPECKER.** If you see a "large" Downy, it will be a Hairy which is 9 inches compared to the Downy's 6 inches. Otherwise they look alike.

Fig. 19. **RED-BELLIED WOODPECKER** (Male). This colorful woodpecker has moved up the East Coast in recent years and now is a regular at many Cape feeders. The male has a lot of red on his head. The belly has a reddish glow during mating season.

Fig. 20. **RED-BELLIED WOODPECKER** (Female). This shows the female with less red on the head.

Fig. 21. **RED-HEADED WOODPECKER.** Though uncommon on the Cape, this photo was taken in Eastham.

Fig. 22. **NORTHERN MOCKINGBIRD.** The Northern Mockingbird comes to the yard to eat berries. It has white wing flashes when it flies, and is very aggressive and protective of its territory.

Fig. 23. **NORTHERN MOCKINGBIRD.** On cold winter days, most birds fluff out their feathers to keep warm. Like the Cardinal and the Tufted Titmouse, the Mockingbird has only recently become a year-round resident of the Cape, previously preferring the warmer climates in the winter.

Fig. 24. **COMMON BOBWHITE** (Male). This chubby ground feeder will come in for cracked corn. Unfortunately they have lost much of their habitat so they stay in larger tracts such as parks and wildlife sanctuaries. The female is buff-colored where the male is white around the head.

Fig. 25. **AMERICAN ROBIN.** There are Robins on the Cape year-round. They are here to eat worms in the warm weather and berries in the cold weather.

Fig. 26. **AMERICAN ROBIN.**
This bird is enjoying juniper berries.

Fig. 27. **CAROLINA WREN.** A delightful bird that has moved up the East Coast, it builds a nest in the most unexpected places and sings very loudly for such a tiny bird.

Fig. 28. **CAROLINA WREN.** During the colder months, this wren will hop on the feeder for food.

Fig. 29. **HOUSE SPARROW.** This is actually a Weaver Finch introduced from Europe, and not the same as our native sparrows. Not a very popular bird; because of its numbers, it pushes out other birds from Cape nesting boxes.

Fig. 30. **HOUSE SPARROW** (immature). This young fellow doesn't look like a pest as it stops to smell the flowers.

Fig. 31. **WHITE-THROATED SPARROW.** This is a tough one to call. This sparrow seems more common in fall and winter, but you can hear its "Sam Peabody-Peabody" call most of the year.

Fig. 32 . **YELLOW-RUMPED WARBLER** (spring) (I still prefer the name Myrtle Warbler.) This pretty warbler is on the Cape in great numbers during the month of May. But . . .

Fig. 33. **YELLOW-RUMPED WARBLER** (fall & winter). You will find them in your yard during the cold months after seed and suet.

Fig. 35. **YELLOW-SHAFTED FLICKER**. The female will find a nest hole in a nearby woods and proceed to go in and make it larger for her coming brood. She entertains us by sticking out her head from time-to-time to see what's going on.

Fig. 34. **YELLOW-SHAFTED FLICKER.** This member of the Woodpecker family comes in for seed and suet during the cold weather.

Fig. 36. **COMMON CROW.** Always nearby if there are sunflower seeds and cracked corn on the ground. They also are in the woods and the fields, and can even be seen on the beaches at low tide

Fig. 37. **EASTERN BLUEBIRD** (Male). It is difficult to categorize this bird for the book. They appear at nest boxes placed in fields, near power lines, and on golf courses, but more and more they are showing up in people's yards, year-round, looking for water and berries..

Fig. 38. **EASTERN BLUEBIRD** (Female). They make an attractive couple and produce an enjoyable "gurgling" sound to each other in their quiet way

Spring & Summer Visitors

Fig. 39. **GRAY CATBIRD**. One of my favorite spring arrivals, it sings happily with abandon. Usually ground feeders, they love the water, grape jelly, and an occasional raisin. Very friendly.

Fig. 40. **BALTIMORE ORIOLE.** Many people put out oranges at the first sign of an oriole, usually hearing them first. Grape jelly also brings in this beautiful bird.

Fig. 41. **BALTIMORE ORIOLE.** It's a real challenge to try to take a portrait shot of an Oriole away from the feeders. The Oriole will usually nest nearby so soon the area will be inundated with young ones.

Fig. 42. **SUMMER TANAGER.** Grape jelly has brought in an unusual visitor to the feeder.

Fig. 43. **COMMON GRACKLE.** Large groups of these black birds will come to the feeders in spring & fall.

Fig. 44. **BROWN-HEADED COW-BIRD.** An unattractive and unpopular bird that can travel in large flocks. The female lays her large eggs in the nest of smaller birds who exhaust themselves trying to feed and raise the large intruder.

Fig. 45. **INDIGO BUNTING**. It is a special spring day when a beautiful Indigo Bunting stops to feed in your yard. This same bird may stop on its return flight in the fall, but it will have changed into a light brown-colored bird.

Fig. 47. **RUFOUS-SIDED TOWHEE** (Female). The Towhee has a very attractive mate

Fig. 46. **RUFOUS-SIDED TO-WHEE** (Male). A ground feeder that is usually seen rustling about in the leaves. Although he continually calls out "chewink," we still call him a Towhee.

Fig. 48. **RUBY-THROATED HUMMINGBIRD.** Feeders with sweet water and flowers with nectar will bring these attractive little birds to the backyard. They are not too difficult to photograph as they hover while feeding..

ig. 49. **RUBY-THROATED HUMMINGBIRD.** They are easy to photograph if you can find where they perch to rest.

Fall and Winter Visitors

Fig. 50. **SLATE-COLORED JUNCO.** The arrival of this small ground-feeder to the yard usually means colder weather and snow are on the way.

Fig. 51. **AMERICAN TREE SPARROW.** A regular visitor to your feeders in the colder months. Note the bill which is dark on top and yellow below.

Fig. 52. **FOX SPARROW.** An attractive rust-colored bird that is larger than the other sparrows. They are not a common visitor, but during the colder months there are several sightings at Cape feeders..

Fig. 52A. **PINE SISKIN.** Used to be a regular visitor but now only casual. Usually seen competing with a Goldfinch at the thistle feeder.

Cape Cod is covered with marshes and ponds, most surrounded by homes. (I read somewhere that there is a pond for every day of the year – 365.) Not all the marshes and ponds are good for birding and many are inaccessible.

My favorite marsh areas are the Wellfleet Bay Wildlife Sanctuary, Harwich Conservation Area, and the Great Marsh in Barnstable.

Most of my pond photos are taken at Mill Pond in Marston Mills, Salt Pond and Siders Pond in Falmouth, Herring Pond in Eastham, Harwich Conservation Area, and Goose Pond in the Wellfleet Bay Wildlife Sanctuary.

Some birding in these areas can be done from the car or an easy walk along the edges. But many require getting into the bulrushes and marsh grass and getting wet.

Two excellent marsh/pond areas that require a boat ride are the Monomoy Islands off Chatham and the Felix Neck Sanctuary on Martha's Vineyard.

Fig. 53. Canada Goose
Fig. 54. Mute Swan
Fig. 55. Mallard (Male)
Fig. 56. Mallard (Female)
Fig. 57. American Black Duck
Fig. 58. Belted Kingfisher
Fig. 59. Great Blue Heron
Fig. 60. Red-Winged Blackbird (Male)
Fig. 61. Red-Winged Blackbird (Female)
Fig. 62. Green Heron
Fig. 63. Black-Crowned Night Heron

Fig. 64. Snowy Egret
Fig. 65. Great Egret
Fig. 66. Glossy Ibis
Fig. 67. Pied-Billed Grebe
Fig. 68. Snow Goose

Sandpiper/Phalarope Family

Fig. 69. Common Snipe
Fig. 70. Greater & Lesser Yellowlegs
Fig. 71. Short-Billed Dowitcher
Fig. 72. Whimbrel
Fig. 73. Willet
Fig. 74. Willet
Fig. 75. Solitary Sandpiper
Fig. 76. Pectoral Sandpiper
Fig. 77. Stilt Sandpiper
Fig. 78. Wilson's Phalarope (Female)
Fig. 79. Wilson's Phalarope (Male)

Elusive Pond and Marsh Birds

Fig. 80. Wood Duck (Male)
Fig. 81. Wood Duck (Female)
Fig. 82. American Bittern
Fig. 83. Least Bittern

Fig. 84. Sharp-Tailed Sparrow

Fig. 85. Swamp Sparrow

Fig. 86. Seaside Sparrow

Fig. 87. Marsh Wren

Fig. 88. Sora

Fig. 89. Virginia Rail

Fig. 90. Clapper Rail

Cold Weather Waterfowl

Fig. 91. Red-Breasted Merganser (Male)

Fig. 92. Red-Breasted Merganser (Female)

Fig. 93. Common Merganser (Male)

Fig. 94. Common Merganser (Female)

Fig. 95. Hooded Merganser (Male)

Fig. 96. Hooded Merganser (Female)

Fig. 97. Lesser Scaup (Male)

Fig. 98. Greater Scaup (Male)

Fig. 99. Scaup (Female)

Fig. 100. American Wigeon (Male)

Fig. 101. Eurasian Wigeon (Male)

Fig. 102. Gadwall (Male)

Fig. 103. Redhead (Male)

Fig. 104. Canvasback (Male)

Fig. 105. Canvasback (Female)

Fig. 106. Ring-Necked Duck (Male)

Fig. 107. Ruddy Duck

Fig. 108. Common Pintail (Pair)

Fig. 109. Northern Shoveler (Male)

Fig. 110. Green-Winged Teal (Male)

Fig. 111. Blue-Winged Teal (Pair)

Fig. 112. American Coot

Fig. 53. **CANADA GOOSE.** This bird now spends year-round in our area. It has actually become a pest. However, they are fun to watch when their young begin to swim.

Fig. 54. **MUTE SWAN.** Like the Canada Goose, the Mute Swan now overcrowds our lakes and ponds.
But they are a beautiful bird to photograph.

Fig. 55. **MALLARD** (Male). Still a common sight on the Cape & Islands, but they seem to be here in fewer numbers.

Fig. 56. **MALLARD** (Female). The female displays her blue speculum.

Fig. 57. **AMERICAN BLACK DUCK.** Although this duck has very dark plumage, it flashes white underwings when flying.

Fig. 58. **BELTED KINGFISHER.** The Cape's best fisherman as he dives headlong into the water to get his meal. Its loud rattle can be heard long before it comes into view.

Fig. 59. **GREAT BLUE HERON.** A beautiful bird who lazily flies over the marshes. An argument could be made that it is the best fisherman. A bird of great patience, it waits silently to grab its meal.

Fig. 61. **RED-WINGED BLACKBIRD** (Female). Much different than her mate in coloring, these birds sit around their chosen ponds and chatter to each other incessantly

Fig. 60. **RED-WINGED BLACKBIRD** (Male). An early arrival, it comes to the marshes in spring to set up and defend a territory for his mate. This bird is often seen in early spring under the feeders with the Grackles.

Fig. 62. **GREEN HERON.** Another spring arrival, this small heron fishes in the marsh grass along the edges of the marsh ponds, always at the ready to snap out and grab a meal. Very common.

Fig. 63. **BLACK-CROWNED NIGHT HERON.** During the spring and summer, flocks of these herons can be seen roosting in the trees around wooded ponds. There are several rookeries around the Cape and the Islands.

Fig. 64. **SNOWY EGRET.** A small white heron with a black bill and yellow "shoes," it is very entertaining as it shuffles its feet to stir up food, then jumps about with its wings flapping, to catch each morsel. It is very common during the summer.

Fig. 65. **GREAT EGRET.** A large white heron with a yellow bill and black "shoes." It is uncommon on the Cape & Islands, but there are several reports of sightings every year.

Fig. 66. **GLOSSY IBIS.** A casual visitor in the spring and fall. This photo was taken in Brewster.

Fig. 68. **SNOW GOOSE.** Where to place this bird in the book? Not seen very often on the Cape, when it is, it is usually in a marsh, such as was the goose in this photo taken at Wellfleet Bay.

Fig. 67. **PIED-BILLED GREBE.** This tiny diver is usually around in early fall. A favorite spot to see it is the Harwich Conservation area.

Sandpiper/Phalarope Family

Fig. 69. **COMMON SNIPE.** A long-billed wader that moves slowly among the marsh grasses. You will need patience to wait until it comes into the open. My photos of this bird are usually at Wellfleet Bay in the fall.

Fig. 70. **GREATER & LESSER YELLOWLEGS.** Very similar in appearance, although different in size, these birds do not usually feed in the same areas. I was pleased to get them together in this photo so we have a comparison. Very common birds for us during the summer season.

Fig. 71. **SHORT-BILLED DOWITCHER.** During the warmer months, this bird is seen both in the marshes and on the beaches. It is shown here because the photo was taken in the Wellfleet Bay marsh.

Fig. 72. **WHIMBREL.** A large sandpiper that is a late summer regular at Wellfleet Bay as it comes in to feed on fiddler crabs.

Fig. 73. **WILLET.** You will know when you are approaching a Willet nesting area in the marsh as this good-sized bird noisily dive-bombs you. Then it will land a few feet away and scold you.

Fig. 74. **WILLET.** A very dull gray bird becomes spectacular in flight with its black and white wing pattern.

Fig. 75. **SOLITARY SANDPIPER.** An uncommon visitor in late summer. My best photos of the Solitary were taken at Wellfleet Bay and the Chatham waste treatment plant.

Fig. 76. **PECTORAL SANDPIPER.** This is another late summer visitor. The striped bib on the breast is a distinct marking.

Fig. 77. **STILT SANDPIPER.** Not a very common visitor, but look closely at groups of Yellowlegs in late summer and you might see the darker-legged Stilt. This photo was taken at Wellfleet Bay.

Fig. 78. **WILSON'S PHALAROPE** (Female). A favorite with women birders, the female Phalaropes have all the beautiful plumage while the males are a much duller coloring. These birds are not a common sighting anymore, at least for me.

Fig. 79. **WILSON'S PHALAROPE** (Male). The male darts back and forth crouched very low over the water searching for food.

Elusive Pond and Marsh Birds

Fig. 80. **WOOD DUCK** (Male). A very beautiful bird if you can find it around the edges of a hidden pond. This photo was taken of a Wood Duck who had a crush on a female Mallard in Sandwich's Shawme Pond, so he was very visible to photograph.

Fig. 81. **WOOD DUCK** (Female). Even more difficult to find with its much duller plumage.

Fig. 82. **AMERICAN BITTERN.** It is amazing how this large bird can remain so well hidden in the marsh grass when only a few feet away from where you're standing.

Fig. 83. **LEAST BITTERN.** A very timid bird that hides in the tall marsh grass. It takes great patience, and a lot of luck, to photograph this one.

Fig. 84. **SHARP-TAILED SPARROW.** A successful view of this sparrow usually results in wet feet. Normally seen in the tall marsh grass running along the edges of creeks.

Fig. 85. **SWAMP SPARROW.** Difficult to find in the marshes but easier to photograph in the fall when this sparrow comes out to eat at vegetable gardens gone to seed.

Fig. 86. **SEASIDE SPARROW.** A most difficult bird to see, let alone photograph. It is a regular in the middle of the Great Marsh in Barnstable but you need a reliable guide to get out there. This photo was taken at Fort Hill in Eastham when a flood tide pushed the birds out to the sides of the marsh.

Fig. 87. **MARSH WREN.** This tiny bird lives at the base of the tall phragmites along the marsh streams. You will hear the "cackle" and they will suddenly pop up, fly a short ways and drop down again. This photo was taken at Fort Hill at the same time as the Seaside Sparrow (Fig. 86).

Fig. 88. **SORA.** A small, chunky rail with a yellow bill. A photo results from a lucky opportunity when the Sora stops in an opening. Note the big feet.

Fig. 89. **VIRGINIA RAIL.** A dark rail about the same size as a Sora and even more secretive. This photo occurred when I was fortunate enough to be present with a person who could "call" this rail out of the reeds. Everyone has some talent.

Fig. 90. **CLAPPER RAIL.** A larger rail that is uncommon to the Cape marshes. I've seen them "called" into view by hitting two stones together.

Cold Weather Waterfowl

Fig. 91. **RED-BREASTED MERGANSER** (Male). A most abundant winter bird that seems to be everywhere there is water. They are also seen in large flocks close to the beaches.

Fig. 92. **RED-BREASTED MERGANSER** (Female). The crested head of this bird can be rather comical especially when it is wet from diving. Males are black and females rusty.

Fig. 93. **COMMON MERGANSER** (Male). Despite its name, this bird is less common than the Red-Breasted or the Hooded. The male's head is a smooth green without a wet crest like the others.

Fig. 94. **COMMON MERGANSER** (Female). To me, this is one of the love-liest of the winter diving ducks.

Fig. 95. **HOODED MERGANSER** (Male). A spectacular little bird with a black and white crown that fans up and down. It is a winter regular at Jemima Pond in Eastham and at Little Pond in Falmouth.

Fig. 96. **HOODED MERGANSER** (Female). A lovely, dainty bird that always looks as if you have just surprised her.

Fig. 97. **LESSER SCAUP** (Male). Seen in Falmouth and other locations in very large flocks in winter. The Lesser and Greater are almost impossible to tell apart unless the sun shows the color on the head. The Lesser has a purple gloss on a more pointed head.

Fig. 98. **GREATER SCAUP** (Male). here you can see the greenish gloss on the more rounded head of the Greater.

Fig. 99. **SCAUP** (Female). I hope the male Scaups can distinguish the Greater Scaup females from the Lesser. I cannot.

Fig. 100. **AMERICAN WIGEON** (Male). Also referred to as the "Baldplate" because of its white top-knot. My best photos of this bird have been taken at Mill Pond in Marston Mills.

Fig. 101. **EURASIAN WIGEON** (Male). Keep looking whenever you see American Wigeons and if you are fortunate you will spot the red-brown head of an Eurasian. Although rare, we usually have one or two each winter in the area.

Fig. 102. **GADWALL** (Male). Becoming more common on the Cape each year. You can identify this attractive duck by its black rump. It is often seen with Wigeons so Mill Pond in Marston Mills is a good photo location.

Fig. 103. **REDHEAD** (Male). An attractive diving duck that I am seeing less and less on the Cape. Most recently it has been at Shivericks Pond in the center of Falmouth.

Fig. 104. **CANVASBACK** (Male). Similar in color to the Red-head but with a longer body and neck. Like the Redhead, the Canvasback numbers seem to be declining on the Cape.

Fig. 105. **CANVASBACK** (Female). Very different in color than the male. This alert young lady seems to be deciding whether to take off or not.

Fig. 106. **RING-NECKED DUCK** (Male). Not that easy to find, but when you do, consider the name of this duck and that it has a ring at the back of the bill, not the neck. It also has a white whale outline on its side.

Fig. 107. **RUDDY DUCK.** A small diving duck with a spiky tail. It is helpless on land because it cannot walk. It is a regular at Herring Pond in Eastham.

Fig. 108. **COMMON PINTAIL** (pair). A beautiful, graceful duck that is getting more difficult for me to find each year. Best chances are at Hallett's Mill Pond in Yarmouthport and at the pond at Felix Neck Sanctuary on Martha's Vineyard.

Fig. 109. **NORTHERN SHOVELER** (Male). A rarer visitor to the Cape but easily recognized by its large spade-like bill. The last time I saw one was in Falmouth.

Fig. 110. **GREEN-WINGED TEAL** (Male). A common winter visitor that prefers the quiet rivers near the marshes. The Harwich Conservation Area is usually a reliable spot to see this small duck.

Fig. 111. **BLUE-WINGED TEAL** (Pair). Not as common as the Green-Winged but they tend to prefer the same locales. I used to see them in the pond near the lighthouse on South Monomoy.

Fig. 112. **AMERICAN COOT.** A fun bird to watch and easily found by its incessant "kuk-kuk-kuk." We used to enjoy watching them try to walk on the ice at Shawme Pond in Sandwich. They are not as common there now as Sandwich has stopped feeding there.

Cape Cod and the Islands are the ideal location for shorebird habitat. They are surrounded by shoreline, have offshore islands and barrier beaches. You can take a whale-watch boat trip and see several species of ocean birds just offshore, in fact you can often see seabirds from the shore off Race Point in Provincetown and Sandy Neck in Barnstable. This habitat has year-round, migratory and rare birds. Monomoy Islands, Martha's Vineyard and Nantucket are famous for their rare species that show up each year.

Fish piers are excellent locations to photograph water birds and it is more comfortable when you can stay in your car and observe during the winter months. My favorite piers are in Provincetown and Wellfleet.

My other favorite seashore locations are:

- National Fish & Wildlife area on Morris Island in Chatham
- Cape Cod Canal in Sandwich
- South Cape Beach in Mashpee
- First Encounter Beach in Eastham
- Wellfleet Bay Wildlife Sanctuary

One of Cape Cod's charms is the long walks along the beaches where we can watch birds in the water, or running along the sand dodging the waves or up among the beach grass on the edge of the dunes. To photograph birds in this environment I recommend a set up including a camp stool so you can sit very quietly until the birds begin to accept your presence. It is best to set up on an incoming tide so that the shore birds will come closer to you as the water rises. Caution: Remember to keep moving the stool back from the water – do not drown.

The Cape is running into serious problems of shared habitat with humans and birds. The Piping Plover, with its camouflage, chooses to nest on the same beaches that attract the summer people. The Terns (Least, Common and Roseate) are conflicting with the much larger Herring and Black-backed Gulls whose numbers continue to grow. The unwillingness to share habitat, as the Cape becomes more crowded, seems to be the heart of the problem.

You can help by not entering a nesting area designated as "Off Limits". If you discover a nest outside a posted area do not keep the bird off the nest by your presence. Use a spotting scope or a long telephoto lens so the nesting birds will not leave the eggs exposed. This same courtesy should be extended to all bird nesting areas wherever you see them.

Among the Dunes and Grasses

Along the beaches are several land birds that live and feed among the dunes and grasses.

Fig. 113. Horned Lark
Fig. 114. Savannah Sparrow
Fig. 115. Water Pipit
Fig. 116. Lapland Longspur
Fig. 117. Snow Bunting
Fig. 118. Snowy Owl

Along the Beaches

The next group includes the birds that run along our beaches, often dodging the waves. The group includes sandpipers, plovers and similar species. Most of these birds leave in the early summer and return in the late summer after nesting further north.

Fig. 119. Least Sandpiper
Fig. 120. Semipalmated Sandpiper
Fig. 121. Spotted Sandpiper
Fig. 122. White-Rumped Sandpiper
Fig. 123. Sanderling
Fig. 124. Purple Sandpiper
Fig. 125. Semipalmated Plover
Fig. 126. Piping Plover
Fig. 127. Piping Plover
Fig. 128. Piping Plover
Fig. 129. Piping Plover
Fig. 130. Black-Bellied Plover
Fig. 131. Black-Bellied Plover
Fig. 132. Golden Plover
Fig. 133. Ruddy Turnstone
Fig. 134. Ruddy Turnstone
Fig. 135. Red Knot
Fig. 136. Red Knot
Fig. 137. Dunlin
Fig. 138. Dunlin

Fig. 139. Hudsonian Godwit
Fig. 140. Hudsonian Godwit
Fig. 141. Marbled Godwit
Fig. 142. American Oystercatcher
Fig. 143. American Oystercatcher
Fig. 144. American Oystercatcher
Fig. 145. Black Skimmer
Fig. 146. Black Skimmer
Fig. 147. Black Skimmer

Gulls and Terns

The Gulls and Terns that are seen on Cape Cod and the Islands.

Fig. 148. Herring Gull
Fig. 149. Herring Gull
Fig. 150. Herring Gull
Fig. 151. Greater Black-Backed Gull
Fig. 152. Ring-Billed Gull
Fig. 153. Laughing Gull
Fig. 154. Laughing Gull
Fig. 155. Laughing Gull
Fig. 156. Bonaparte's Gull
Fig. 157. Bonaparte's Gull
Fig. 158. Glaucous Gull

Fig. 159. Iceland Gull
Fig. 160. Black-Headed Gull
Fig. 161. Lesser Black-Backed Gull
Fig. 162. Little Gull
Fig. 163. Black-Legged Kittiwake
Fig. 164. Black-Legged Kittiwake
Fig. 165. Common Tern
Fig. 166. Common Tern
Fig. 167. Least Tern
Fig. 168. Roseate Tern
Fig. 169. Roseate Tern
Fig. 170. Artic Tern
Fig. 171. Forster's Tern
Fig. 172. Black Tern

Sea Ducks

The sea ducks were principally photographed around the area's fish piers.

Fig. 173. Common Eider (Male)
Fig. 174. Common Eider (Female)
Fig. 175. Bufflehead (Male)
Fig. 176. Bufflehead (Female)
Fig. 177. Common Goldeneye (Male)
Fig. 178. Common Goldeneye (Female) .

Fig. 179. Common Loon
Fig. 180. Common Loon
Fig. 181. Red-Throated Loon
Fig. 182. White-Winged Scoter
Fig. 183. White-Winged Scoter
Fig. 184. Black Scoter
Fig. 185. Surf Scoter
Fig. 186. Scoter (Female)
Fig. 187. Oldsquaw
Fig. 188. Oldsquaw
Fig. 189. Harlequin Duck
Fig. 190. Dovekie
Fig. 191. Thick-Billed Murre
Fig. 192. Thin-Billed Murre
Fig. 193. Horned Grebe
Fig. 194. Red-Necked Grebe
Fig. 195. Razorbill
Fig. 196. Brant
Fig. 197. Double-Crested Cormorant
Fig. 198. Great Cormorant

Seabirds

A birder coming to Cape Cod must plan to include a whale-watch cruise so they can see the seabirds that remain offshore. It is also a treat to see the magnificent whales.

Among the Dunes and Grasses

Fig. 199. Northern Gannet

Fig. 200. Northern Gannet

Fig. 201. Greater Shearwater

Fig. 202. Greater Shearwater

Fig. 203. Sooty Shearwater

Fig. 204. Wilson's Storm Petrel

Fig. 205. Pomarine Jaeger

Fig. 206. Pomarine Jaeger

Fig. 113. **HORNED LARK.** Very common year-round in the dunes and beach grass, it spends most of its time running on the sand and flies only a short distance when disturbed. How this little bird survives the winter wind that blows the sand at a fierce pace is a miracle.

Fig. 114. **SAVANNAH SPARROW.** Another bird that runs on the sand in the beach grass. I do not see it very often in the winter.

Fig. 115. **WATER PIPIT.** A casual visitor that runs along the dunes and beach grass in summer and early fall.

Fig. 116. **LAPLAND LONGSPUR.** I have had only one opportunity to photograph this bird; it was in Brewster at Crosby Landing in February 1990. They share similar habitat with the Horned Larks and Water Pipits.

Fig. 117. **SNOW BUNTING.** These little birds come in small flocks in late fall and winter and add flashes of white as they whirl from one spot to another. Look for them in the deserted beach parking lots.

Fig. 118. **SNOWY OWL.** The word goes out when one of these spectacular birds is spotted along the beaches and the birders go out to get a look. Unfortunately, it usually requires a walk along a cold winter beach, but it can be worth it.

Along the Beaches

Fig. 119. **LEAST SANDPIPER.** The smallest of the "peeps" is very common on our beaches. It is darker brown than the other sandpipers and has greenish legs.

Fig. 120. **SEMIPALMATED SANDPIPER.** Usually seen with the Least Sandpiper, it is lighter in color and has a black bill and legs. This photo shows one investigating the "left-overs" from a digger of clams and quahogs.

Fig. 121. **SPOTTED SANDPIPER.** A small sandpiper that teeters up and down as it runs along the edge of the water.

Fig. 122. **WHITE-RUMPED SANDPIPER.** Most of my photos of this bird were taken on North Monomoy. It has a white rump which can be seen when it's flying. Note that the wing tips extend beyond the tail.

Fig. 123. **SANDERLING.** More common on our beaches in the fall, this is a plump, active bird that races up and down the sand like a wind-up toy. Note the eyes watching me even if they are about to snooze.

Fig. 124. **PURPLE SANDPIPER.** This dark sandpiper is seen more in late fall as it climbs over rocks and jetties. I've found it to be a most difficult bird to get close to and photograph.

Fig. 125. **SEMIPALMATED PLOVER.** An abundant little shorebird. It is one of the easiest to photograph as it tends to come up close to check on you, especially at low tide.

Fig. 126. **PIPING PLOVER.** This is one of the Cape's endangered species that all serious birders try to protect. Its sandy color works against it, camouflaging it from humans. This timid little bird arrives in early spring, scrapes a nest and lays its eggs in the sand on the beaches that will become the most populated in the summer.

Fig. 127. **PIPING PLOVER.** When people arrive for the summer with their off-road vehicles and dogs, they cannot see this bird and its eggs (can you see the four eggs in this photo?) Volunteers set up fences and flags around the nesting areas, but it only works if people honor the signals.

Fig. 128. **PIPING PLOVER.** If you disturb any beach nesting bird, get out of the way fast, so you don't keep them off the eggs for any length of time. They will quickly return to protect the eggs from the sun.

Fig. 129. **PIPING PLOVER.** Here's a youngster starting out on its own.

Fig. 130. **BLACK-BELLIED PLOVER.** Very abundant in large flocks especially on the islands off the coast of Chatham. It wears a very black breast in the summer and fall, but it begins to fade as winter approaches.

Fig. 132. **GOLDEN PLOVER.** Look closely at the large flocks of Black-Bellied Plovers and you may find a wandering Golden. Their brown coloring stands out from their black and white relatives.

Fig. 131. **BLACK-BELLIED PLOVER.** The younger ones in the late fall have no black belly at all.

Fig. 133. **RUDDY TURNSTONE.** A chunky, colorful shorebird that drops by regularly in late summer to do exactly what its name implies; it turns over stones on the beach.

Fig. 134. **RUDDY TURNSTONE.** A younger bird very interested in an empty seashell.

Fig. 135. **RED KNOT.** A stocky shorebird that wears bright colors in early summer when it stops by in large flocks.

Fig. 136. **RED KNOT.** I think the silver markings on this bird in the fall are more beautiful than any other shorebird.

Fig. 137. **DUNLIN.** A few Dunlins stop in the spring on their way north. They have a rusty colored back and a black patch across the belly.

Fig. 138. **DUNLIN.** But when flocks of Dunlins return in the fall they are a much duller gray bird. This is a wonderful shorebird to photograph because it will let you get quite close. Note the slightly down-curved bill.

Fig. 139. **HUDSONIAN GODWIT.** A large shorebird with a long, slightly upturned thin bill. North Monomoy Island has a flat muddy area that is called "Godwit Bar" because it is a regular summer stopping place for this bird.

Fig. 140. **HUDSONIAN GODWIT.** I am including this photo so you can see the long wingspan and the white wing markings.

Fig. 141. **MARBLED GODWIT.** It is a special day when you can pick out a beautiful Marbled Godwit among the Hudsonians. It is a larger bird than its relatives and is a lovely buff-brown with a long upturned bill.

Fig. 142. **AMERICAN OYSTERCATCHER.** Now here is an easy bird to identify, with its large orange bill, yellow eye, orange eye-ring and pink legs. This unusual arrangement is accompanied by a very noisy "wheep."

Fig. 144. **AMERICAN OYSTERCATCHER.** A few nest on the Monomoy Islands. Here is a small group discussing the latest news.

Fig. 143. **AMERICAN OYSTERCATCHER.** A photo that shows off the large white wings.

Fig. 145. **BLACK SKIMMER.** An occasional nester on the Monomoy Islands.

Fig. 146. **BLACK SKIMMER.** Here is a youngster just beginning to grow into its bill.

Fig. 147. **BLACK SKIMMER.** The Skimmer's unusual red bill is specially designed so they can fish on the fly.

Gulls and Terns

Fig. 148. **HERRING GULL.** The most numerous gull on the Cape and considered a messy pest. Now that the landfills have cleaned up their act, the gull depends on fishermen and scraps left by humans.

Fig. 149. **HERRING GULL.** The most pleasing photos of this bird are taken as they are soaring against a blue sky.

Fig. 150. **HERRING GULL.** Here's a youngster letting its parents know that it is hungry!

Fig. 151. **GREATER BLACK-BACKED GULL.**
This large bird with a large bill is one of my least
favorites. I've seen it perform too many acts of cruelty.

Fig. 152. **RING-BILLED GULL.** This gull is one of my favorites. It is
a smaller gull and one who begs from you at the beach if you are eating a
sandwich... even in your car. Taking a photo with water as a background
can really enhance your picture.

Fig. 153. **LAUGHING GULL.** This gull migrates with the Cape Codders who spend the cold weather in Florida and returns with them in the fall. This photo was taken at a nesting site on new Island in Nauset Marsh.

Fig. 154. **LAUGHING GULL.** A young bird near the nest site shown in Fig. 153.

Fig. 155. **LAUGHING GULL.** Living up to its name.

Fig. 156. **BONAPARTE'S GULL.** Although this gull has a black head in the summer, we only see it in its winter plumage when it arrives in late fall. All that's left is a black dot behind the eye.

Fig. 157. **BONAPARTE'S GULL.** This lucky shot was taken as the bird was swallowing its meal at the Wellfleet Fish Pier. But it does show the beautiful wing markings.

Fig. 158. **GLAUCOUS GULL.** A large chalky white gull that is an uncommon winter visitor. This photo was taken at the Chatham Fish Pier as the gull floated by on a small ice floe.

Fig. 159. **ICELAND GULL.** A pretty white gull that is an occasional winter visitor. Although they seem more common on the coast north of Boston, we do see them once in a while on the Cape.

Fig. 160. **BLACK-HEADED GULL.** Rather a rare sighting on the Cape, this photo was taken in the Wellfleet Pier parking lot with many other common gulls. Fortunately we spotted the distinctive red bill and red legs.

Fig. 161. **LESSER BLACK-BACKED GULL.** A smaller version of the Greater, it is not easy to locate because there may be only one in a huge group of the common gulls. The more yellow legs are an identifying feature.

Fig. 162. **LITTLE GULL.** I had only seen this bird once flying over a whale-watch boat with its black under wings helping us to identify it. But just as the book said, we found this smallest gull on the beach with a group of Bonaparte's Gulls.

Fig. 163. **BLACK-LEGGED KITTIWAKE.** These gulls are usually seen flying over the water along the Cape beaches.

Fig. 164. **BLACK-LEGGED KITTIWAKE.** The black-tipped wings are the best identifying mark.

Fig. 165. **COMMON TERN.** A very common summer nester on the islands off Cape Cod, it is shown among some of the Cape's beautiful beach habitat.

Fig. 166. **COMMON TERN.** Sometimes the competition can be fierce on the Cape.

Fig. 167. **LEAST TERN.** The smaller tern on a nest behind a tiny piece of driftwood. Note the white visor that identifies this bird. This tern has been very successful nesting at West Dennis beach.

Fig. 168. **ROSEATE TERN.** This beautiful bird has become seriously endangered on the Cape. Its nesting sites have been taken over by the larger gulls. They have retreated to Bird Island in Buzzards Bay where last year they were threatened by an oil spill. Tough life for a little bird.

Fig. 169. **ROSEATE TERN.** Here's a young bird stretching its wings on North Monomoy.

Fig. 170. **ARCTIC TERN.** A few pairs nest on Cape Cod but it is the most southernly point of its range. To me this is one of the most beautiful of all birds with its long silvery wings and deep red bill.

Fig. 171. **FORSTER'S TERN.** A late summer visitor to the Cape beaches. It is usually in winter plumage with the black patch through the eye.

Fig. 172. **BLACK TERN.** A rare sighting for me, this photo was taken on North Monomoy in June 1986.

Sea Ducks

Fig. 173. **COMMON EIDER** (Male). These birds winter around the Cape in huge flocks. The best places to see them are Corporation Beach in Dennis and at the Sandwich end of the Cape Cod Canal.

Fig. 174. **COMMON EIDER** (Female). The female is a golden brown bird with distinctly outlined feathers.

Fig. 175. **BUFFLEHEAD** (Male). I refer to this little diving duck as the "Chickadee of the sea." It is always on the move, bouncing over and under the water.

Fig. 176. **BUFFLEHEA**D (Female). The males and females are usually seen in small flocks. They are often seen on island ponds and lakes.

Fig. 177. **COMMON GOLDENEYE** (Male). One of the most common diving ducks, this lovely green-headed bird is easily seen near the shore and from fish piers.

Fig. 178. **COMMON GOLDENEYE** (Female). The female is a brown bird but has the bright golden eye of her mate.

Fig. 180. **COMMON LOON.** But this loon is a very common winter visitor and can be seen from most beaches. At this time it has lost its brilliant black and white plumage.

Fig. 179. **COMMON LOON.** This loon can be a rare summer visitor in full plumage. This photo was taken in August in Chatham's Stage Harbor.

Fig. 181. **RED-THROATED LOON.** A very regular winter visitor, it is seen in the same locales as the Common Loon. The longer neck and lighter color identify it from the Common.

Fig. 182. **WHITE-WINGED SCOTER.** Not the most attractive bird, but this duck is a winter regular in fairly large flocks. The "comma" through the eye and the white wing patch when it flies are the key identifying features.

Fig. 183. **WHITE-WINGED SCOTER.** This close-up photo was taken of a bird that struggled over the sand to sit next to me on a sandbar where I was set up to photograph.

Fig. 184. **BLACK SCOTER.** This chunky black bird carries an orange bump on its bill.

Fig. 185. **SURF SCOTER.** Easily identified by its black and white head. All three scoters hang out together off the Cape beaches but the White-Winged is the most numerous.

Fig. 186. **SCOTER** (Female). All three females of the Scoter family are very similar. I think the head markings indicate that this is a female Surf Scoter.

Fig. 187. **OLDSQUAW.** A very attractive bird with a long thin tail. Its light color identifies it among the other winter diving ducks.

Fig. 188. **OLDSQUAW.** Although it is considered a winter bird on the Cape, a few show up in the summer such as this one photographed in July off Morris Island in Chatham.

Fig. 189. **HARLEQUIN DUCK.** Usually you have to view this beautiful duck from the shore as it dives among the ocean breakers. Nauset Beach in Orleans is a regular winter spot. This photo was taken of a very cooperative duck who came into the Wellfleet Fish Pier.

Fig. 190. **DOVEKIE.** This tiny ocean bird, who rarely comes near land, has selected the Wellfleet Fish Pier to visit the last few years.

Fig. 191. **THICK-BILLED MURRE.** Another ocean bird that is occasionally seen in the winter at Macmillan Wharf in Provincetown.

Fig. 192. **THIN-BILLED MURRE.** Sometimes seen with the Thick-Billed, this bird is identified by the black line from the eye down over the cheek.

Fig. 193. **HORNED GREBE.** Usually seen in the waters off the beaches, but every so often one will come into a fish pier. How about that eye like a red jewel.

Fig. 194. **RED-NECKED GREBE.** The largest grebe is identified by its long neck. Just like the Horned Grebe, photo opportunities will occur at the Cape fish piers.

Fig. 195. **RAZORBILL.** I have photographed this ocean bird off Macmillan Wharf, but never very close. This photo was taken of an injured bird at Wellfleet Bay Sanctuary about to be released.

Fig. 196. **BRANT.** A goose with black head and neck. Usually found in large flocks feeding in the water near the beaches. Abundant in winter on Cape Cod Bay and Nantucket Sound.

Fig. 197. **DOUBLE-CRESTED CORMORANT.** This is our summer Cormorant identified by its orange throat. It becomes a pest after fishing all day then sitting on a boat or on telephone wires over a pond and spending the night. Needless to say they cause a mess.

Fig. 198. **GREAT CORMORANT.** This is our winter Cormorant identified by its white throat. Both Cormorants dive for fish and then dry their wings as shown in this photo.

Seabirds

Fig. 199. **NORTHERN GANNET.** A large white seabird that flies over the ocean and then suddenly dives into the water out of sight. It usually comes up with a fish. This activity can be seen not only from a boat, but also from land, especially when the white bird banks and shows its black wing tips.

Fig. 200. **NORTHERN GANNET.** This youngster was photographed at Wellfleet Fish Pier after a storm had brought them in from the sea.

Fig. 201. **GREATER SHEARWATER.** This will be the Shearwater that is most easily seen on a whale watching trip. Notice this bird putting on its brakes to go after some food.

Fig. 203. **SOOTY SHEARWATER.** This dark bird shows how gracefully the shearwaters fly with their wing tips almost touching the water.

Fig. 202. **GREATER SHEARWATER.** A rather rare close-up photo taken on a visit to Bird Island in Buzzards Bay.

Fig. 204. **WILSON'S STORM PETREL.** A small black bird with a white rump patch. It is abundant just offshore in the summer. It skims over the waves and seems to dance on the water while feeding.

Fig. 205. **POMARINE JAEGER.** This is definitely an ocean bird that you usually only see flying over the boat at top speed. It harasses gulls and terns in flight until they drop their food and the jaeger grabs it. I had never had a photo opportunity, but I received a call that one was at Dowses Beach in Osterville. Here it is sitting on the breakwater.

Fig. 206. **POMARINE JAEGER.** He was near a fisherman who was fishing with squid as bait, which he tossed periodically for the Jaeger. The fisherman was unaware that he had created this rare photo opportunity.

v. Fields (Managed Lands)

Fields have become the rarest habitat on Cape Cod and the Islands. Almost all the farms are gone and the open fields have become so valuable that most have been sold for development.

The areas that I use to photograph the birds that require these open lands are:

- Crane Reservation on Route 151 in Falmouth
- Fort Hill in Eastham
- Wellfleet Bay Wildlife Sanctuary
- Ram Pasture on Nantucket
- Felix Neck Wildlife Sanctuary on Martha's Vineyard
- Pilgrim Heights in Truro (for hawk migrations)

It is unfortunate that this habitat is disappearing. There is no more beautiful sight than to see birds among the wildflowers in an open field, with Bobwhites on stone walls, birds on fences and hawks lazily circling overhead looking for voles and mice.

Fig. 207. Tree Swallow
Fig. 208. Tree Swallow
Fig. 209. Barn Swallow
Fig. 210. Barn Swallows
Fig. 211. Rough-Winged Swallow
Fig. 212. Eastern Kingbird
Fig. 213. Western Kingbird

Fig. 214. Eastern Meadowlark
Fig. 215. Bobolink
Fig. 216. Bobolink
Fig. 217. Cedar Waxwing
Fig. 218. Cedar Waxwing
Fig. 219. Bohemian Waxwing
Fig. 220. Purple Finch (Male)
Fig. 221. Purple Finch (Female)
Fig. 222. House Wren
Fig. 223. American Woodcock
Fig. 224. Common Redpoll
Fig. 225. Northern Shrike
Fig. 226. Rusty Blackbird
Fig. 227. Rusty Blackbird
Fig. 228. European Starling
Fig. 229. Ring-Necked Pheasant
Fig. 230. Upland Sandpiper
Fig. 231. Grasshopper Sparrow
Fig. 232. Vesper Sparrow

Hawks & Similar Species

The habitats of the Cape and Islands includes fields that attract hawks and similar species where they can fly and search for food.

Fig. 233. Red-Tailed Hawk
Fig. 234. Red-Tailed Hawk
Fig. 235. Northern Harrier (Female)
Fig. 236. Northern Harrier (Male)
Fig. 237. Sharp-Shinned Hawk
Fig. 238. Sharp-Shinned Hawk
Fig. 239. Cooper's Hawk
Fig. 240. American Kestrel
Fig. 241. American Kestrel
Fig. 242. Broad-Winged Hawk
Fig. 243. Broad-Winged Hawk
Fig. 244. Rough-Legged Hawk
Fig. 245. Rough-Legged Hawk
Fig. 246. Osprey
Fig. 247. Osprey
Fig. 248. Short-eared Owl
Fig. 249. Turkey Vulture
Fig. 250. Turkey Vulture
Fig. 251. Peregrine Falcon
Fig. 252. Merlin
Fig. 253. Northern Goshawk

Sparrow & Others at Harvest Time

In late September and October, there is a large vegetable garden in Truro that goes to seed, and the birds flock there to partake of the harvest. The next few photos show the variety of Sparrows that come plus a couple other regulars. I've presented a one-hour slide show of just the birds at this garden.

Fig. 254. Song Sparrow
Fig. 255. Savannah Sparrow
Fig. 256. White-Throated Sparrow
Fig. 257. Field Sparrow
Fig. 258. White-Crowned Sparrow
Fig. 259. White-Crowned Sparrow (Young)
Fig. 260. Swamp Sparrow
Fig. 261. Lincoln Sparrow
Fig. 262. Lark Sparrow
Fig. 263. Clay-Colored Sparrow
Fig. 264. Dickcissel
Fig. 265. Indigo Bunting
Fig. 266. Blue Grosbeak

Fig. 207. **TREE SWALLOW.** An abundant bird in spring through early fall, it will be seen gliding round and round, over fields and ponds gathering insects. They nest in bird boxes and tree holes. Their white breast tells them apart from other swallows.

Fig. 208. **TREE SWALLOW.** In October they begin to gather in masses as they get ready to migrate south.

Fig. 209. **BARN SWALLOW.** This little bird prefers to nest in barns along the beams. They make mud nests to hold the eggs. Unfortunately, there are not many barns left on the Cape that keep a window open for these swallows. I know they have some success at horse stables, but they improvise wherever they can find beams in outside buildings.

Fig. 210. **BARN SWALLOWS.** The young ones leave the nest early so they are still looking to be fed as they sit on the branches. Here we see the "Andrews Sisters" singing "Feed Me" to the approaching adults.

Fig. 211. **ROUGH-WINGED SWALLOW.** This brown swallow makes its nest in river banks, sand dunes, and anywhere it can find an appropriate spot. I've seen them coming out between cement blocks and under storage trailers. You can see where it gets its name as you look under the top of the wing in this picture.

Fig. 212. **EASTERN KINGBIRD.** Seen regularly in the summer flitting back and forth in the fields chasing insects. After every short flight it sits motionless on a branch or a weed waiting for its next opportunity. A very aggressive bird for its size, it even goes after hawks to protect its territory.

Fig. 213. **WESTERN KINGBIRD.** An occasional visitor to the Cape, usually seen in the same area as the Eastern Kingbird.

Fig. 214. **EASTERN MEADOWLARK.** This yellow-breasted ground feeder prefers to hide in tall grass so is difficult to photograph. They suddenly fly up and then down in the grass again. The best photo opportunity is when the bird lands on a post or on top of a tree to sing.

Fig. 215. **BOBOLINK.** The Bobolink makes a brief spring stop as a black bird. It sings a happy, bubbling song as it flies from one grassy spot to another.

Fig. 216. **BOBOLINK.** It returns for a brief fall visit, but this time as a striped buff-colored bird. Hard to believe one bird could change plumage this much.

Fig. 217. **CEDAR WAXWING.** Very unpredictable as it flies in small flocks looking for berries, it can stop next door and wipe out your neighbor's bushes and you won't see a one.

Fig. 218. **CEDAR WAXWING.** I think this regal bird is one of the most beautiful we get to see.

Fig. 219. **BOHEMIAN WAXWING.** An occasional wanderer to the Cape especially during a snowy spell when the winter berries are important to the Waxwings. Rusty around the face and under the tail, this bird stands out amongst the Cedar Waxwings.

Fig. 220. **PURPLE FINCH** (Male). This used to be a regular visitor at backyard feeders but apparently has been pushed out by more aggressive birds. Sometimes confused with the House Finch, the Purple Finch is a much more overall red bird.

Fig. 221. **PURPLE FINCH** (Female). Very different looking from her mate, we do see her more often than the male on the Cape. Look for the Purple Finches at the top of evergreens in a field singing their happy song.

Fig. 222. **HOUSE WREN.** Not as abundant as the Carolina Wren, but they are here. One pair has nested in the same box at Wellfleet Bay for the past few years. Like the tiny Carolina Wren, it has a loud voice that you'd expect from a much larger bird.

Fig. 223. **AMERICAN WOODCOCK.** It takes a very lucky opportunity to photograph a Woodcock in daylight. There are several mating sites on the Cape and Islands where you can watch their aerial antics, but it occurs at dusk. This photo was taken in January just before a snowstorm.

Fig. 224. **COMMON REDPOLL.** Nowhere near as abundant as they used to be on the Cape, we did have a few at our feeder in a recent winter during a period of zero weather. This photo was taken in 1997 in a field at Crosby Landing in Brewster.

Fig. 225. **NORTHERN SHRIKE.** An occasional visitor from the North during the colder weather, this photo was taken in February at Fort Hill. It looks like a Mockingbird from a distance, but a closer look shows the black mask and hooked bill.

Fig. 226. **RUSTY BLACKBIRD.** This photo was taken in May and shows this bird as black with a pale yellow eye.

Fig. 227. **RUSTY BLACKBIRD.** This photo was taken in October and now the bird has changed to its rusty plumage.

Fig. 228. **EUROPEAN STARLING.** An introduced species from Europe and now widespread in the United States. An unpopular bird because it travels in huge flocks which can cover your yard looking for food. A test for a photographer, take a pleasing picture of a Starling.

Fig. 229. **RING-NECKED PHEASANT.** A spectacular bird to see and exciting to photograph. This bird has been introduced to the Cape as a game bird for hunters. This practice has been cut back recently so we don't see as many Pheasants. This photo was taken by the side of the road into Morris Island in Chatham.

Fig. 230. **UPLAND SANDPIPER.** The Upland Sandpiper requires open fields with managed grass. This photo was taken on an assignment to locate and photograph this elusive bird. I went on a guided tour of Otis Air Field Base where we counted nine in the fields.

Fig. 231. **GRASSHOPPER SPARROW.** This is truly a shy, elusive bird. The only reliable location I know of is the Crane Reservation in Falmouth. Move very quietly, listen for the thin high buzzing song, and then try to locate the bird.

Fig. 232. **VESPER SPARROW.** Another sparrow that prefers fields. Look for the white on each side of its tail feathers when it flies. A closer look will show the white eye-ring. Has a pretty song similar to a Song Sparrow.

Hawks & Similar Species

Fig. 234. **RED-TAILED HAWK.** It's always nice to get a shot of a hawk in flight.

Fig. 233. **RED-TAILED HAWK.** This is the Cape's most common hawk and is fairly easy to photograph. They sit on open branches, posts, and, as in this case, light fixtures. The band across the breast is the best identifying feature because the red tail is not always visible.

Fig. 235. **NORTHERN HARRIER** (Female). You will see this beautiful hawk flying lazily over fields and marshes just above the ground. Look for the bright white rump patch when it's flying.

Fig. 236. **NORTHERN HARRIER** (Male). I've seen this spectacular hawk many times, but a close-up photo continues to elude me. That's what makes bird photography exciting, to pursue the perfect shot of these beautiful creatures, like this gray hawk with black wing tips.

Fig. 237. **SHARP-SHINNED HAWK.** This bird's favorite meal is the smaller songbirds. They used to have to search for them and chase them over fields and in the woods. But now we have put out feeders, so just as we go to the store to get chicken, this hawk just waits patiently at our feeders.

Fig. 238. **SHARP-SHINNED HAWK.** Each spring we have an excellent hawk-watching opportunity at Pilgrim Heights in Truro. One of the most frequent sightings is the "Sharpy" which will burst right out on top of you as it skims the tree tops.

Fig. 239. **COOPER'S HAWK.** A larger version of the Sharp-Shinned with the same eating habits, although they tend to take larger birds. The Cooper's long tail is rounded at the ends while the Sharp-Shinned's tail is squared.

Fig. 240. **AMERICAN KESTREL.** A very colorful falcon that, until recently, was very common on the Cape. Lately my sightings are few and far between.

Fig. 241. **AMERICAN KESTREL.** They are very fond of crickets and grasshoppers and can hover over a field for a few minutes with rapid wing beats waiting to dive on its prey.

Fig. 242. **BROAD-WINGED HAWK.** This young fellow is perched on a branch in Provincetown. We can see this hawk usually flying, not sitting.

Fig. 243. **BROAD-WINGED HAWK.** One of the regulars that fly over Pilgrim Heights during the spring migration. Note the bands on the tail.

Fig. 244. **ROUGH-LEGGED HAWK.** We tend to see this hawk in the colder weather in February or March. I was trying to photograph this bird, which was perched on a telephone pole, from my Jeep. He was very accommodating as he flew down and sat next to me.

Fig. 245. **ROUGH-LEGGED HAWK.** A spectacular bird in flight with its beautiful wing patterns.

Fig. 246. **OSPREY.** The Osprey has made a strong comeback on the Cape and Islands. They begin building nests in the spring aided by volunteers who have erected poles with crossbars. The nests remain from year to year and get larger as more sticks are added each spring.

Fig. 247. **OSPREY.** A beautiful bird as it flies around the nest or dives into the water for fish. This photo shows an Osprey that believes I have come too close.

Fig. 248. **SHORT-EARED OWL.** A bird of the open country often seen hunting during the daylight hours. This photo was taken of a very cooperative subject who sat for me at sunset at First Encounter Beach in Eastham.

Fig. 249. **TURKEY VULTURE.** Not a pretty bird when you get a close look.

Fig. 250. **TURKEY VULTURE.** It is a much more attractive bird as it soars overhead looking for a meal.

Fig. 251. **PEREGRINE FALCON.** Because it flies at such high speeds, you must wait until this falcon is sitting for a good look. This photo was taken at the entrance to Pilgrim Heights during the hawk migration. It is as if the bird decided to be a welcome sign to the area.

Fig. 252. **MERLIN.** Although there are several reported sightings every year on the Cape, this is the only photo opportunity I've ever had of a Merlin. The photo was taken in April 1997 at First Encounter in Eastham.

Fig. 253. **NORTHERN GOSHAWK.** I've only seen this hawk on the Cape a few times, mostly at Wellfleet Bay.

Sparrow & Others at Harvest Time

Fig. 254. **SONG SPARROW.** Sitting on a wire used for tomato plants, this is the most abundant sparrow there.

Fig. 255. **SAVANNAH SPARROW.** A close-up of a post sitter.

Fig. 256. **WHITE-THROATED SPARROW.** A very common garden visitor.

Fig. 257. **FIELD SPARROW.** A regular visitor with its pink bill and legs.

Fig. 258. **WHITE-CROWNED SPARROW.** Only a few adults show up at the garden.

Fig. 259. **WHITE-CROWNED SPARROW** (Young). Many young White-Crowns are present during this fall event.

Fig. 260. **SWAMP SPARROW.** A very common regular. This close-up clearly shows the gray breast and the rust on the upper wing.

Fig. 261. **LINCOLN SPARROW.** This rather uncommon Sparrow is easily seen at the garden each fall.

Fig. 266. **BLUE GROSBEAK.** We do not get many Blue Grosbeaks in the spring in their blue plumage, but several return to the garden in the fall as a light brown bird.

The most difficult habitat to see and photograph birds is among the trees, especially when the leaves are out. You must situate yourself so you can observe bare branches and the ends of limbs. Birds tend to be curious and want to see where they are going next before they fly to another spot. Be patient, but be prepared when your subject pops into view.

My favorite forest areas are:

+ Beech Forest in Provincetown (for the warbler migration in May)
+ Along the river at Wellfleet Bay Wildlife Sanctuary
+ Harwich Conservation Area
+ White Cedar Swamp at Marconi Area in Wellfleet
+ Punkhorn Area in Brewster

One of the more difficult photographic challenges is to take clear pictures of warblers as they migrate through the trees in early May. Whether you are using binoculars or a camera, time your birding in the forests to late April or early May so that you can see better before the leaves are in full bloom. It seems that the smaller birds are in the thickest woods. Warblers, kinglets, vireos and gnatcatchers are all in the 4 to 6 inch size and are in constant motion. A serious birder needs to learn the bird songs so they can identify what's in an area before they see the bird.

Fig. 267. Great-Horned Owl
Fig. 268. Great-Horned Owl
Fig. 269. Great-Horned Owlet
Fig. 270. Great-Horned Owlets
Fig. 271. Common Screech Owl
Fig. 272. Common Screech Owl
Fig. 273. Common Screech Owl
Fig. 274. Saw-Whet Owl
Fig. 275. Long-eared Owl
Fig. 276. Bald Eagle
Fig. 277. Bald Eagle (Immature)
Fig. 278. Red-Shouldered Hawk
Fig. 279. Ruffed Grouse
Fig. 280. Wild Turkey
Fig. 281. Wild Turkey
Fig. 282. Common Nighthawk
Fig. 283. Yellow-Bellied Sapsucker
Fig. 284. Brown Creeper
Fig. 285. Winter Wren
Fig. 286. Brown Thrasher
Fig. 287. Hermit Thrush
Fig. 288. Veery
Fig. 289. Wood Thrush
Fig. 290. Swainson's Thrush
Fig. 291. Gray-Cheeked Thrush
Fig. 292. Rose-Breasted Grosbeak (Male)
Fig. 293. Rose-Breasted Grosbeak (Female)
Fig. 294. Scarlet Tanager (Male)

Fig. 295. Scarlet Tanager (Female)
Fig. 296. Summer Tanager
Fig. 297. Summer Tanager (Immature)
Fig. 298. Great Crested Flycatcher
Fig. 299. Great Crested Flycatcher
Fig. 300. Least Flycatcher
Fig. 301. Yellow-Bellied Flycatcher
Fig. 302. Willow Flycatcher
Fig. 303. Orchard Oriole (Male)
Fig. 304. Orchard Oriole (Female)
Fig. 305. Orchard Oriole(First Year)
Fig. 306. Yellow-Billed Cuckoo
Fig. 307. Black-Billed Cuckoo

Small Species

Now we come to the most challenging group of birds to photograph. They are tiny (from 4 inches to 6 inches), they flit constantly after insects, they are often hidden by branches and leaves and they are only here a few days as they migrate North to nest. There are a few exceptions that I'll point out as we go along. A perfect May morning for me is an early arrival at the Beech Forest, followed by a stop at Pilgrim Heights to see how the hawk migration is going, then an afternoon at Wellfleet Bay. A southwest wind also helps.

Fig. 308. Blue-Gray Gnatcatcher
Fig. 309. Ruby-Crowned Kinglet
Fig. 310. Golden-Crowned Kinglet
Fig. 311. Eastern Phoebe
Fig. 312. Eastern Wood Pewee
Fig. 313. Red-Eyed Vireo
Fig. 314. Solitary Vireo
Fig. 315. White-Eyed Vireo
Fig. 316. Warbling Vireo
Fig. 317. Yellow-Rumped Warbler

Fig. 318. Pine Warbler
Fig. 319. Yellow Warbler
Fig. 320. Prairie Warbler
Fig. 321. Black & White Warbler
Fig. 322. Palm Warbler
Fig. 323. Black-Throated Green Warbler
Fig. 324. Black-Throated Blue Warbler
Fig. 325. Black-Throated Blue Warbler
Fig. 326. Northern Parula Warbler
Fig. 327. American Redstart (Male)
Fig. 328. American Redstart (Female)
Fig. 329. American Redstart (Female)
Fig. 330. Magnolia Warbler
Fig. 331. Chestnut-Sided Warbler
Fig. 332. Blackpoll Warbler
Fig. 333. Canada Warbler
Fig. 334. Blackburnian Warbler
Fig. 335. Nashville Warbler

Rarer Warblers

The next few Warblers are much less common on the Cape; when one is seen it causes some excitement.

Fig. 336. Cape May Warbler
Fig. 337. Wilson's Warbler
Fig. 338. Bay-Breasted Warbler
Fig. 339. Blue-Winged Warbler
Fig. 340. Kentucky Warbler
Fig. 341. Tennessee Warbler
Fig. 342. Hooded Warbler
Fig. 343. Prothonotary Warbler
Fig. 344. Yellow-Throated Warbler
Fig. 345. Cerulean Warbler

Fig. 346. Golden-Winged Warbler

There are four other Warbler species that go by non-Warbler names.

Fig. 347. Common Yellowthroat (Male)
Fig. 348. Common Yellowthroat (Female)
Fig. 349. Ovenbird
Fig. 350. Northern Waterthrush
Fig. 351. Yellow-Breasted Chat

Fig. 267. **GREAT-HORNED OWL.** Our most common owl, they build their nests high up in pine trees, under the canopy, so the crows do not see them as easily.

Fig. 268. **GREAT-HORNED OWL.** It takes a good spotter to find the nest, but when you do, look around the area to find the male watching guard.

Fig. 269. **GREAT-HORNED OWLET.** When you know their habitat area, you can expect to see the young owls learning to fly. You can be led to the location of an owl by following the harassing cries of crows and blue jays.

Fig. 270. **GREAT-HORNED OWLETS.** A real treat is to find twins looking down at you from a nearby branch.

Fig. 271. **COMMON SCREECH OWL.** We have a tree in Brewster that has been a home for a Screech Owl several times. I photographed this red phase owl in that tree.

Fig. 272. **COMMON SCREECH OWL.** The next day, the tree cavity was filled with a gray phase owl.

Fig. 273. **COMMON SCREECH OWL.** On the third day, they were both out sunning themselves.

Fig. 274. **SAW-WHET OWL.** This tiny owl is very difficult to find, but when you do locate one, it usually watches you so you can take pictures.

Fig. 275. **LONG-EARED OWL.** Usually hiding in heavy underbrush near the trunk of a tree, it takes great patience to work your way around into a clear photo opportunity.

Fig. 276. **BALD EAGLE.** The adult Bald Eagle is an occasional visitor to the Cape in the colder weather. It is seen flying over deep woods where there are ponds, such as Nickerson State Park in Brewster. This photo was taken on the roof of the Visitor's Center in Provincetown.

Fig. 277. **BALD EAGLE** (Immature). The younger eagles are seen a little more frequently than the adult. This young fellow was photographed at Rock Harbor in Orleans.

Fig. 278. **RED-SHOULDERED HAWK.** I have not seen many Red-Shouldered Hawks on the Cape. This photo was taken near the Orleans Yacht Club where this bird showed up regularly a few years ago.

Fig. 279. **RUFFED GROUSE.** I have to admit that I've never seen a Ruffed Grouse in the deep woods where it hangs out. This lucky shot was taken from my Jeep as the bird walked along the side of the road.

Fig. 280. **WILD TURKEY.** There have been lots of sightings of Wild Turkeys on the Cape in the last few years. Before then we had to go to Felix Neck on Martha's Vineyard to see one.

Fig. 281. **WILD TURKEY.** We got a chuckle when a lady from Truro called Wellfleet Bay to report that she had two unwise turkeys in her yard on Thanksgiving morning...just like Pilgrim times.

Fig. 282. **COMMON NIGHTHAWK.** I was very fortunate to come upon this bird sitting on a branch in the Beech Forest in Provincetown.

Fig. 283. **YELLOW-BELLIED SAPSUCKER.** I usually include this bird in my slide shows for audiences that are not avid birders. I think they need to know there really is a bird by this name. The best place for me to see this bird is at Wellfleet Bay.

Fig. 284. **BROWN-CREEPER.** You must photograph this tiny bird from the side or it disappears in camouflage if it is back-to against the trunk of the tree. It lands at the bottom of a tree and climbs upwards.

Fig. 285. **WINTER WREN.** Now here is a real photographer's challenge. This tiny dark brown ball of feathers spends its time foraging on the ground in the woods.

Fig. 286. **BROWN THRASHER.** We're just not seeing as many of these handsome birds lately. They are excellent camera subjects because they are curious and come out in the open if you imitate its call by "kissing" the back of your hand. Catbirds and Mockingbirds respond in the same manner.

Fig. 287. **HERMIT THRUSH.** Look for this thrush to be hunting on the ground among the leaves. We have seen them at backyard feeders on cold winter days.

Fig. 288. **VEERY.** This thrush is seen on the Cape during the spring migration, especially in the Beech Forest in Provincetown.

Fig. 289. **WOOD THRUSH.** A common visitor in the warmer weather as it breeds in the area. However this has been a very frustrating subject for me as I never can seem to get it out in the open for a clear picture.

Fig. 290. **SWAINSON'S THRUSH.** Another spring migrant that stops briefly on its way north to breed. The buff eye-ring is a good identifying feature.

Fig. 291. **GRAY-CHEEKED THRUSH.** Seen at the same time and in the same places as the Swainson's, the gray cheeks and the lack of the eye-ring are the only ways to tell them apart.

Fig. 292. **ROSE-BREASTED GROSBEAK** (Male). One of the most beautiful birds of the spring migration.

Fig. 293. **ROSE-BREASTED GROSBEAK** (Female). A very different looking bird from her mate, she actually looks more like a large sparrow.

Fig. 294. **SCARLET TANAGER** (Male). A beautiful spring migrant with the most brilliant scarlet plumage.

Fig. 295. **SCARLET TANAGER** (Female). Who would guess that the brilliant male would have a yellow-colored mate?

Fig. 296. **SUMMER TANAGER.** A rare spring visitor to the Cape, the male is completely red, but not as brilliant as the Scarlet Tanager. The female is also a yellow-colored bird.

Fig. 297. **SUMMER TANAGER** (Immature). This youngster showed up in the Beech Forest in May 1985 and gave me many opportunities to photograph it.

Fig. 298. **GREAT CRESTED FLYCATCHER.** A very common visitor during the warmer months as it nests in our woods. It makes a loud "wheep" very often so you'll know it's around.

Fig. 299. **GREAT CRESTED FLYCATCHER.** There have been several examples of the bird coming into yards and even using nesting boxes if they are near the woods.

Fig. 300. **LEAST FLYCATCHER.** There are five small flycatchers that are referred to as Empidonax that are so similar they are very difficult to identify in the field. The Least is the most common and I believe this photo shows the Least because of its lighter gray color.

Fig. 301. **YELLOW-BELLIED FLYCATCHER.** Another Empidonax which can be identified in a photo when this bird's yellow-belly is seen.

Fig. 302. **WILLOW FLYCATCHER.** The only other Empidonax in our area is the Willow and it can only be identified by its song, a rather sneezy sounding "fitz-bew." The bird in this photo was clearly making that sound as I took the picture.

Fig. 303. **ORCHARD ORIOLE** (Male). Occasionally this Oriole will come into your yard to check out an orange, but most of the time it stays in the edges of the woods.

Fig. 304. **ORCHARD ORIOLE** (Female). As is mostly the case with orioles and tanagers, the female is a yellowish bird.

Fig. 305. **ORCHARD ORIOLE** (First Year). This young male displays the black bib which he'll wear even as he turns the red color of his father. He has happily discovered an oriole feeder at Wellfleet Bay.

Fig. 306. **YELLOW-BILLED CUCKOO.** As you can see, the two cuckoos that come to the Cape to breed, are well-named. The bright yellow bill and large white spots under the tail, seen when flying, are the identifying features of this cuckoo.

Fig. 307. **BLACK-BILLED CUCKOO.** Here the black bill is plainly seen. It is a mixed blessing to see these two cuckoos on the Cape; if you see lots of them, it usually means we have lots of caterpillars, but the cuckoos go to work and try to eat as many as they can.

Small Species

Fig. 308. **BLUE-GRAY GNATCATCHER.** It was a few years before I finally got a good picture of this little body of constant motion. It is one of the earliest spring arrivals so the leaves are not yet fully out.

Fig. 309. **RUBY-CROWNED KINGLET.** The added challenge here is to have the head in a position so that the ruby crown shows.

Fig. 310. **GOLDEN-CROWNED KINGLET.** I had real trouble trying to get a close-up of this little fellow. Finally was successful in getting this shot.

Fig. 311. **EASTERN PHOEBE.** One of the spring arrivals that stays around the Cape to nest.

Fig. 312. **EASTERN WOOD PEWEE.** It always feels as if you're spelling this bird's name wrong. Another Cape nester.

Fig. 313. **RED-EYED VIREO.** A bird that sings all the time as it bounces among the trees. You can see how the photography gets tougher as the green begins to appear on the trees. The maps indicate that the Red-Eye nests in this area.

Fig. 314. **SOLITARY VIREO.** This is the earliest arriving Vireo and you can see how clear it shows on a leafless branch.

Fig. 315. **WHITE-EYED VIREO.** Not a common sighting on the Cape as this Vireo prefers to breed south of here. Fortunately, I've been able to photograph it at Wellfleet Bay. This Vireo has a very distinct song that lets you know if it's in the area.

Fig. 316. **WARBLING VIREO.** Not an easy bird to find and photograph, it does warble, but not very loudly. Its coloring is quite drab. But I finally got this shot in the Beech Forest parking lot.

Fig. 317. **YELLOW-RUMPED WARBLER.** I included the Yellow-Rumped in the section for "In and Around Your Yard" but it has to be included here too because it is so abundant in the woods during the migration.

Fig. 318. **PINE WARBLER.** You can hear this bird before you see it. It is a trill similar to the Chipping Sparrow. The Pine Warbler is a year-round bird on the Cape so we can see its yellow plumage in the winter too.

Fig. 319. **YELLOW WARBLER.** Another Warbler that nests on the Cape. This photo is probably of a female because the rusty breast streaks are so faint.

Fig. 320. **PRAIRIE WARBLER.** You can hear the song of the Prairie Warbler as it "zees" right up the musical scale during the summer months. This means that it is a summer nester here. This photo is probably of a male because the chestnut stripes can be seen on the back.

Fig. 321. **BLACK & WHITE WARBLER.** One of the first arrivals in the spring, it climbs up and down trees near the trunk.

Fig. 322. **PALM WARBLER.** – another early arrival which you can see helps a photographer because the leaves are not yet out. You can recognize this bird as its tail continually bobs up and down.

Fig. 323. **BLACK-THROATED GREEN WARBLER.**
A regular visitor in the spring . I often wondered why the name "Green" was included for this bird, but it is described as having an olive-green crown.

Fig. 324. **BLACK-THROATED BLUE WARBLER.**
The combination of black and blue make it difficult to get a clear photo of this bird. The light has to be just right.

Fig. 325. **BLACK-THROATED BLUE WARBLER.**
This female warbler showed up at a feeder in Brewster in
January 2001. Very unusual.

Fig. 326. **NORTHERN PARULA
WARBLER.** A regular spring visitor usually
in pretty good numbers. This is such a
beautiful bird.

Fig. 327. **AMERICAN REDSTART** (Male). Another colorful visitor that is very common in the spring. The bright orange patches really stand out as he flits among the trees.

Fig. 328. **AMERICAN REDSTART** (Female). A female warbler that competes with the male for beauty.

Fig. 329. **AMERICAN REDSTART** (Female). She is especially beautiful when she fans her tail.

Fig. 330. **MAGNOLIA WARBLER.** A lovely combination of black, yellow and white, especially the black necklace on the yellow breast. The Magnolia has a yellow rump patch similar to the Yellow-Rumped Warbler.

Fig. 331. **CHESTNUT-SIDED WARBLER.** A colorful bird with a yellow cap and a black patch through the eye. A later arrival causes interference with leaves as you try to get a clear photo.

Fig. 332. **BLACKPOLL WARBLER.** A very late arrival makes this bird a tough subject to photograph. In general it is similar to the Black and White Warbler, but the head is more similar to a Black-Capped Chickadee.

Fig. 333. **CANADA WARBLER.** A late arrival in fewer numbers, this bird has a necklace similar to the Magnolia and the eye-ring is very prominent.

Fig. 334. **BLACKBURNIAN WARBLER.** Although they do not visit in great numbers, the bright orange is a welcome sight amongst the leaves.

Fig. 335. **NASHVILLE WARBLER.** The white eye-ring and the yellow breast help identify this warbler.

Rarer Warblers

Fig. 336. **CAPE MAY WARBLER.** A very colorful bird that was quite common when I started birding on the Cape, but it has been a rare sighting in recent years.

Fig. 337. **WILSON'S WARBLER.** I do see a Wilson's almost every year, but only one or two. It is constant motion, but rather cute when it sits and cocks its head to one side.

Fig. 338. **BAY-BREASTED WARBLER.** Like the Wilson's, I see one or two of this Warbler each year, but as you can see from this photo, it visits the Cape when there is heavy foliage on the trees.

Fig. 339. **BLUE-WINGED WARBLER.** A yellow bird with blue-gray wings and a black line through the eye. Although this photo was taken at Wellfleet Bay, I usually have to go off-Cape to Moose Hill in Sharon to see this Warbler.

Fig. 340. **KENTUCKY WARBLER.** I photographed this Warbler on the Silver Spring path at Wellfleet Bay on May 10, 1992. I never saw the bird again until May 10, 2002 at almost the exact same spot.

Fig. 341. **TENNESSEE WARBLER.** A very drab Warbler and very difficult to see as it darts amongst the leaves.

Fig. 342. **HOODED WARBLER.** An exciting find for me. I had the opportunity to photograph it in the Beech Forest parking lot.

Fig. 343. **PROTHONOTARY WARBLER.** My wife Corinne spotted this bird on the Silver Spring trail at Wellfleet Bay several years ago. She came running back to say she'd seen a very different Warbler. So, I had an opportunity to photograph this spectacular golden bird that usually stays south of the Cape. I've only seen it once since at the Beech Forest.

Fig. 344. **YELLOW-THROATED WARBLER.** One of the Cape's premier birders called me on New Year's Day in 1986 to tell me he had this Warbler at his front yard feeders. So, I packed my gear and my rather crude blind and set up in his front yard and was rewarded by this photo of a rare Cape visitor. His neighbors still talk about the strange New Years Day sight of me on a cold morning in a blind in Harwich.

Fig. 345. **CERULEAN WARBLER.** This photo was taken back in my beginning days when I didn't know the birds' identification very well. I was calmly photographing this rare bird when members of the Cape Cod Bird Club came by and became very excited at what I was looking at. I've only seen this Warbler once since.

Fig. 346. **GOLDEN-WINGED WARBLER.** A May 1988 afternoon on the Silver Spring trail at Wellfleet Bay is the only time I have ever seen this Warbler. It popped out in front of me and I took one quick shot before it flew away. That is a good example of the excitement of bird photography.

Fig. 347. **COMMON YELLOWTHROAT** (Male). A very common visitor to the Cape during the warmer months. You can see why I refer to this bird as the Lone Ranger.

Fig. 348. **COMMON YEL-LOWTHROAT** (Female). This young lady is building a nest at Wellfleet Bay.

Fig. 349. **OVENBIRD.** Although it is a regular summer visitor, it is well camouflaged as it rustles in the leaves on the ground. Listen for his song "Teacher, Teacher, Teacher" and it will help you find him.

Fig. 350. **NORTHERN WATERTHRUSH.**
This is another difficult to find bird as it runs along
the edges of streams and wet woods.

Fig. 351. **YELLOW-BREASTED CHAT.** This photo of
the largest Warbler was a quick shot taken on Morris Island
in September 1982. This is the only sighting I've had on the
Cape. I have traveled several times during the colder months
to the area behind the Falmouth Town Hall where this bird
is often reported to be – but I miss it every time.

One of the real joys of bird photography is to receive a call that a rare sighting has occurred somewhere on the Cape and Islands. The challenge of getting there before it leaves and getting a good photo is very exciting. But I must admit that I've grown older and the thought of packing all my gear and getting to Katama on Martha's Vineyard in 2005 and fighting for a spot to photograph the Bird of the Century was just too much for me. So, I do not have a photo of the Red-footed Falcon. However, I hope you enjoy looking back to see some of the rare birds I've photographed.

Let me digress for a minute and tell you that when I first purchased my serious photo equipment, I joined a very competitive camera club. The desire to improve for your peers to judge can be quite obsessive. Soon I learned that scenic photos put you up against the majority of photographers. My first step to specialize was to photograph butterflies, which turned out to be very interesting, but the season was too short. That's when I discovered birds and the challenge to get good pictures. At that time, I knew nothing about birds, so I sent my photos to Mass Audubon where a wonderful expert named Dick Forster "adopted" me and not only identified my birds, but mentored and encouraged me to continue. About a year after the focus on birds, Corinne called me at work (a very unusual event in itself) and said there was a different bird at our feeders. I came home, photographed the bird and later sent the slide to Dick. Well, to say the least, it caused a bit of a flurry as Mass. Audubon sent Dave Clapp from Moose Hill to confirm the sighting. A Brambling had flown all the way from Europe to our little backyard in Mansfield, Massachusetts. I took this as a sign that maybe I was supposed to be a bird photographer.

Fig. 352. Brambling
Fig. 353. White-Winged Dove
Fig. 354. Fork-Tailed Flycatcher

Fig. 355. Ruff
Fig. 356. Fulvous Whistling Duck
Fig. 357. Reef Heron
Fig. 358. Chilean Flamingo
Fig. 359. Thayer's Gull
Fig. 360. Long-Billed Curlew
Fig. 361. Northern Wheatear
Fig. 362. Sprague's Pipit
Fig. 363. Sandhill Crane
Fig. 364. Spotted Redshank
Fig. 365. Rock Wren
Fig. 366. Ash-Throated Flycatcher
Fig. 367. Western Tanager
Fig. 368. Painted Bunting (Male)
Fig. 369. Painted Bunting (Female)
Fig. 370. Scissortail Flycatcher
Fig. 371. White Pelicans
Fig. 372. Black-Tailed Godwit
Fig. 373. Mountain Bluebird
Fig. 374. Townsend's Solitaire
Fig. 375. Mississippi Kite
Fig. 376. Bar-Tailed Godwit
Fig. 377. Lark Bunting
Fig. 378. Eurasian Kestrel
Fig. 379. Magnificent Frigatebird
Fig. 380. Calliope Hummingbird
Fig. 381. Western Tanager

Fig. 352. **BRAMBLING.** This turned out to either be the first, or close to the first, sighting of this bird in Massachusetts. The photo was taken in March 1979.

Fig. 353. **WHITE-WINGED DOVE.** July 1980, Wellfleet Bay.

Fig. 354. **FORK-TAILED FLYCATCHER.** September 1981, Chatham.

Fig. 355. **RUFF.** July 1982, Wellfleet Bay.
A Reeve was also present.

Fig. 356. **FULVOUS WHISTLING DUCK.** August 1983, South Monomoy. I was with a group of birders from Wellfleet Bay led by Bob Prescott. To keep out of their way, I went the opposite direction and was the only one to have this sighting. Of course, I didn't know what I had seen until my Mass. Audubon friends identified them.

Fig. 357. **REEF HERON.** August 1983, Nantucket. This is an example of what a photographer goes through when there is a major bird sighting. When I arrived there were at least two or three hundred birders lined up with spotting scopes and binoculars. Those of us who had cameras wanted so badly to get closer, but a photographer who tries to sneak out closer in front of all these people and spooks the bird is a very unpopular person as the bird flies away. At least you can see the white cheek and the yellow feet.

Fig. 358. **CHILEAN FLAMINGO.** August 1985, North Monomoy. You can see by the spots on the lens that this was taken on a rainy day.

Fig. 359. **THAYER'S GULL.** February 1986, Chatham Fish Pier. I would have had no idea this was a rare sighting, but fortunately Blair Nikula was present.

Fig. 360. **LONG-BILLED CURLEW.** June 1987, Nauset Marsh at Coast Guard Beach. This was a difficult bird to find although I knew it was there. Nauset Marsh is so big and the Curlew seemed to blend in.

Fig. 361. **NORTHERN WHEATEAR.** October 1988, Red River Beach in Harwich. I photographed another Wheatear at Fort Hill in Eastham in October 1995.

Fig. 362. **SPRAGUE'S PIPIT.** December 1988, Provincetown Airport. This little bird really blended in and was tough to find. My wife finally got it in front of her and slowly moved it in my direction. It sometimes takes teamwork.

Fig. 363. **SANDHILL CRANE.** May 1990, Provincetown Airport. I have photographed the Sandhill Crane two times since then, once in Provincetown in 2002 and again in Barnstable in 2004.

Fig. 364. **SPOTTED REDSHANK.** August 1990, Wellfleet Bay. Bob Prescott sent someone to get me while I was exhibiting my work in Orleans, to be sure we had a photo of this rare visitor.

Fig. 365. **ROCK WREN.** November 1991, South Orleans.

Fig. 366. **ASH-THROATED FLYCATCHER.**
December 1991, Wellfleet Bay.

Fig. 367. **WESTERN TANAGER.** February
1992, in a backyard in Eastham.

Fig. 368. **PAINTED BUNTING** (Male).
January 1993, at a feeder in Brewster

Fig. 369. **PAINTED BUNTING** (Female).
February 1993, at a feeder near Fort Hill in Eastham.

Fig. 370. **SCISSORTAIL FLYCATCHER.** October 1993, at Fort Hill in Eastham.

Fig. 371. **WHITE PELICANS.** November 1993, on Bump's River in Centerville.

Fig. 372. **BLACK-TAILED GODWIT.** June 1994, at Wellfleet Bay. This was probably the most cooperative rare bird as it would come and pose in front of me to have his portrait taken.

Fig. 373. **MOUNTAIN BLUEBIRD.** January 1995, at the National Seashore Headquarters in Wellfleet.

Fig. 374. **TOWNSEND'S SOLITAIRE.** January 1997, West Barnstable.

Fig. 375. **MISSISSIPPI KITE.** June 1997, Orleans. There is excitement when this Kite is seen occasionally flying high in the sky during the spring migration. It was very exciting when this fellow landed in an area at the end of Giddiah Hill Road in Orleans.

Fig. 376. **BAR-TAILED GODWIT.** January 1998, Plymouth. I hope this isn't considered cheating because this photo was taken at a non-Cape Plymouth beach. But it was so close I'm sure we could have seen Cape Cod from where we were.

Fig. 377. **LARK BUNTING.** April 2000, North Truro. I got a real close-up when this bird landed near me, but a branch across the eye ruined the picture.

Fig. 378. **EURASIAN KESTREL.** May 2002, Morris Island Causeway.

Fig. 379. **MAGNIFICENT FRIGATEBIRD.** September 2002, taken over Chatham Light on a rainy day.

Fig. 380. **CALLIOPE HUMMINGBIRD.** January2003, North Eastham. It is a miracle not only how it got here, but that it survived. The owner of the property had a barn and she kept the top door open with a feeder at the opening so this tiny creature had food and protection.

Fig. 381. **WESTERN TANAGER.** January 2004, Brewster. I had to include this bird even though we showed a Western Tanager as a 1992 sighting. Twenty-five years after our first rare sighting in our backyard in Mansfield, Massachusetts, this Western Tanager brought birders from all over New England to our backyard in Brewster, where it sat on our feeder during one of the coldest spells in Cape history.

VIII. Closing Words

Expertise

Birding is a popular pastime on Cape Cod and there are many resources for both residents and visitors. Consult the local newspapers for bird walks led by members of the Cape Cod Bird Club. They are also an excellent source of information on rare birds in the area. They meet on the second Monday every month (September through May) at 7:30pm at the Cape Cod Museum of Natural History in Brewster.

Check out the Cape Cod Museum of Natural History and the Massachusetts Audubon Sanctuaries in Falmouth (Ashumet), Martha's Vineyard (Felix Neck) and Wellfleet Bay for programs and bird walks.

The National Fish and Wildlife Headquarters on Morris Island in Chatham has information about birding on the Monomoy Islands and South Beach.

Finally, a must for anyone coming to Cape Cod to bird is the newly updated *Birding Cape Cod* published by the Cape Cod Bird Club & Massachusetts Audubon Society.

Conclusion

In closing I'd like to say a few things about birding. It will usually take you out in the fresh air, hopefully to enjoy the sunshine and to beautiful areas to look for birds. Unless it is a very rare bird, it will take you to less crowded places, even in July and August. But you will meet some of the most friendly people who are very willing to share the birds they've seen and where they've seen them. Come out and join us.

Roger S. Everett
Brewster, Cape Cod
July 2005

Note: Numbers refer to figure numbers.

BITTERN, American, 82
    Least, 83
BLACKBIRD, Red-winged, 60, 61
    Rusty, 226, 227
BLUEBIRD, Eastern, 37, 38
    Mountain, 373
BOBOLINK, 215, 216
BOBWHITE, Common, 24
BRAMBLING, 352
BRANT, 196
BUFFLEHEAD, 175, 176
BUNTING, Indigo, 45, 265
    Lark, 377
    Painted, 368, 369
    Snow, 117
CANVASBACK, 104, 105
CARDINAL, Northern, 3, 4, 5
CATBIRD, Gray, 39
CHAT, Yellow-breasted, 351
CHICKADEE, Black-capped, 1, 2
COOT, American, 112
CORMORANT, Double-crested, 197
    Great, 198
COWBIRD, Brown-headed, 44
CRANE, Sandhill, 363
CREEPER, Brown, 284
CROW, American, 36
CUCKOO, Black-billed, 307
    Yellow-billed, 306
CURLEW, Long-billed, 360
DICKCISSEL, 264
DOVE, Mourning, 9
    White-winged, 353
DOVEKIE, 190

DOWITCHER, Short-billed, 71
DUCK, American Black, 57
    Fulvous Whistling, 356
    Harlequin, 189
    Ring-necked, 106
    Ruddy, 107
    Wood, 80, 81
DUNLIN, 137, 138
EAGLE, Bald, 276, 277
EGRET, Great, 65
    Snowy, 64
EIDER, Common, 173, 174
FALCON, Peregrine, 251
FINCH, House, 7, 8
    Purple, 220, 221
FLAMINGO, Chilean, 358
FLICKER, Common, 34, 35
FLYCATCHER, Ash-throated, 366
    Fork-tailed, 354
    Great Crested, 298, 299
    Least, 300
    Scissor-tailed, 370
    Willow, 302
    Yellow-bellied, 301
FRIGATEBIRD, Magnificent, 379
GADWALL, 102
GANNET, Northern, 199, 200
GNATCATCHER, Blue-gray, 308
GODWIT, Bar-tailed, 376
    Black-tailed, 372
    Hudsonian, 139, 140
    Marbled, 141
GOLDENEYE, Common, 177, 178
GOLDFINCH, American, 10, 11, 12

GOOSE, Canada, 53
    Snow, 68
GOSHAWK, Northern, 253
GRACKLE, Common, 43
GREBE, Horned, 193
    Pied-billed, 67
    Red-necked, 194
GROSBEAK, Blue, 266
    Rose-breasted, 292, 293
GROUSE, Ruffed, 279
GULL, Black-headed, 160
    Bonaparte's, 156, 157
    Glaucous, 158
    Greater Black-backed, 151
    Herring, 148, 149, 150
    Iceland, 159
    Laughing, 153, 154, 155
    Lesser Black-backed, 161
    Little, 162
    Ring-billed, 152
    Thayer's, 359
HARRIER, Northern, 235, 236
HAWK, Broad-winged, 242, 243
    Cooper's, 239
    Red-shouldered, 278
    Red-tailed, 233, 234
    Rough-legged, 244, 245
    Sharp-shinned, 237, 238
HERON, Black-crowned Night, 63
    Great Blue, 59
    Green, 62
    Reef, 357
HUMMINGBIRD, Calliope, 380
    Ruby-throated, 48, 49

IBIS, Glossy, 66
JAEGER, Pomarine, 205, 206
JAY, Blue, 6
JUNCO, Slate-colored, 50
KESTREL, American, 240, 241
        Eurasian, 378
KILLDEER, 230A
KINGBIRD, Eastern, 212
        Western, 213
KINGFISHER, Belted, 58
KINGLET, Golden-crowned, 310
        Ruby-crowned, 309
KITE, Mississippi, 375
KITTIWAKE, Black-legged, 163, 164
KNOT, Red, 135, 136
LARK, Horned, 113
LONGSPUR, Lapland, 116
LOON, Common, 179, 180
        Red-throated, 181
MALLARD, 55, 56
MEADOWLARK, Eastern, 214
MERGANSER, Common, 93, 94
        Hooded, 95, 96
        Red-breasted, 91, 92
MERLIN, 252
MOCKINGBIRD, Northern, 22, 23
MURRE, Thick-billed, 191
        Thin-billed, 192
NIGHTHAWK, Common, 282
NUTHATCH, Red-breasted, 16
        White-breasted, 14, 15
OLDSQUAW, 187, 188
ORIOLE, Baltimore, 40, 41
        Orchard, 303, 304, 305
OSPREY, 246, 247
OVENBIRD, 349
OWL, Common Screech, 271, 272, 273
        Great Horned, 267, 268, 269, 270
        Long-eared, 275
        Saw-whet, 274
        Short-eared, 248
        Snowy, 118

OYSTERCATCHER, American, 142, 143, 144
PELICAN, White, 371
PETREL, Wilson's Storm, 204
PEWEE, Eastern, 312
PHALAROPE, Wilson's, 78, 79
PHEASANT, Ring-necked, 229
PHOEBE, Eastern, 311
PINTAIL, Common, 108
PIPIT, Sprague's, 362
      Water, 115
PLOVER, Black-bellied, 130, 131
        Lesser Golden, 132
        Piping, 126, 127, 128, 129
        Semipalmated, 125
RAIL, Clapper, 90
      Virginia, 89
RAZORBILL, 195
REDHEAD, 103
REDPOLL, Common, 224
REDSHANK, Spotted, 364
REDSTART, American, 327, 328, 329
ROBIN, American, 25, 26
RUFF, 355
SANDERLING, 123
SANDPIPER, Least, 119
        Pectoral, 76
        Purple, 124
        Semipalmated, 120
        Solitary, 75
        Spotted, 121
        Stilt, 77
        Upland, 230
        White-rumped, 122
SAPSUCKER, Yellow-bellied, 283
SCAUP, Greater, 98
      Lesser, 97
SCOTER, Black, 184
        Surf, 185, 186
        White-winged, 182, 183
SHEARWATER, Greater, 201, 202
      Sooty, 203
SHOVELER, Northern, 109

SHRIKE, Northern, 225
SISKIN, Pine, 52A
SKIMMER, Black, 145, 146, 147
SNIPE, Common, 69
SOLITAIRE, Townsend's, 374
SORA, 88
SPARROW, American Tree, 51
        Chipping, 284A
        Clay-colored, 263
        Field, 257
        Fox, 52
        Grasshopper, 231
        House, 29, 30
        Lark, 262
        Lincoln's, 261
        Savannah, 114, 255
        Seaside, 86
        Sharp-tailed, 84
        Song, 254
        Swamp, 85, 260
        Vesper, 232
        White-crowned, 258, 259
        White-throated, 31, 256
STARLING, European, 228
SWALLOW, Barn, 209, 210
        Rough-winged, 211
        Tree, 207, 208
SWAN, Mute, 54
TANAGER, Scarlet, 294, 295
        Summer, 42, 296, 297
        Western, 367, 381
TEAL, Blue-winged, 111
        Green-winged, 110
TERN, Arctic, 170
        Black, 172
        Common, 165, 166
        Forster's, 171
        Least, 167
        Roseate, 168, 169
THRASHER, Brown, 286
THRUSH, Gray-cheeked, 291
        Hermit, 287

Swainson's, 290
Wood, 289
TITMOUSE, Tufted, 13
TOWHEE, Rufous-sided, 46, 47
TURKEY, Wild, 280, 281
TURNSTONE, Ruddy, 133, 134
VEERY, 288
VIREO, Red-eyed, 313
    Solitary, 314
    Warbling, 316
    White-eyed, 315
VULTURE, Turkey, 249, 250
WARBLER, Bay-breasted, 338
    Black & White, 321
    Blackburnian, 334
    Blackpoll, 332
    Black-throated Blue, 324, 325
    Black-throated Green, 323
    Blue-winged, 339
    Canada, 333
    Cape May, 336
    Cerulean, 345
    Chestnut-sided, 331
    Golden-winged, 346
    Hooded, 342
    Kentucky, 340
    Magnolia, 330
    Nashville, 335
WARBLER, Northern Parula, 326
    Palm, 322

Pine, 318
Prairie, 320
Prothonotary, 343
Tennessee, 341
Wilson's, 337
Yellow, 319
Yellow-rumped, 32, 33, 317
Yellow-throated, 344
WATERTHRUSH, Northern, 350
WAXWING, Bohemian, 219
    Cedar, 217, 218
WHEATEAR, Northern, 361
WHIMBREL, 72
WIGEON, American, 100
    Eurasian, 101
WILLET, 73, 74
WOODCOCK, American, 223
WOODPECKER, Downy, 17
    Hairy, 18
    Red-bellied, 19, 20
    Red-headed, 21
WREN, Carolina, 27, 28
    House, 222
    Marsh, 87
    Rock, 365
    Winter, 285
YELLOWLEGS, Greater, 70
    Lesser, 70
YELLOWTHROAT, Common, 347, 348

Upper Cape & Islands

Bourne
Sandwich
① ②
③
Dennis
④
Barnstable
Yarmouth
⑧
Mashpee
Hyannis
⑪
⑦
⑫
Falmouth
⑤
⑥

1 • Shawme Pond
2 • Sandy Neck Beach
3 • Great Marshes
4 • Hallett's Mill Pond
5 • Salt and Siders Ponds
6 • South Cape Beach
7 • West Dennis Beach
8 • Swan Pond
9 • Felix Neck Wildlife Sanctuary
10 • Rams Pasture
11 • Ashumet Holly Reservation
12 • Crane Reservation

① ② ③
Provincetown
④
Truro
Wellfleet
⑤
⑥
⑦
Eastham
⑧
⑨
⑩
Orleans
⑪
Brewster
⑭
Harwich
Chatham
⑯
⑮ ⑰
⑫
⑬

1 • Race Point Beach
2 • Beech Forest
3 • Pilgrim Heights
4 • Corn Hill
5 • Wellfleet Fish Pier
6 • Wellfleet Bay Wildlife Sanctuary
7 • Coast Guard Beach
8 • First Encounter Beach
9 • Fort Hill
10 • Rock Harbor
11 • Nauset Beach
12 • Morris Island
13 • Monomoy Islands
14 • Chatham Fish Pier
15 • Cockle Cove
16 • Harwich Conservation Area
17 • South Beach

⑨
Martha's Vineyard

⑩
Nantucket

⑬

Lower Cape